MARIO KART 7

PRIMA Official Game Guide
Written by Nick von Esmarch

Prima Games
An Imprint of Random House, Inc.

3000 Lava Ridge Court, Suite 100
Roseville, CA 95661
www.primagames.com

Table of Contents

How to Use This Guide

Welcome to the *Mario Kart 7: Prima Official Game Guide*! We've got a lot of ground to cover, so let's get started.

Introduction

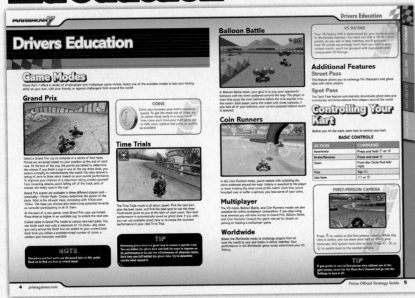

From basic controls to characters and karts, this section aims to prepare you for the tight turns and close races that await you. With a bit of studying, you'll be an expert before you set a tire on the track!

Drivethrough

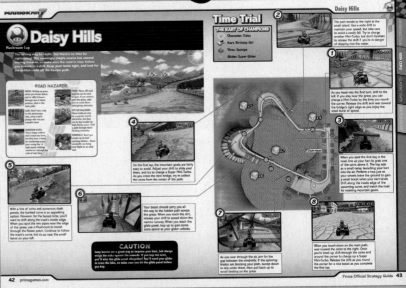

The Drivethrough provides maps and tactics for each of the game's 32 courses. Learn the fastest way around the track, then find out what to expect when you're facing competition. This section is fairly complicated, so there's a detailed introduction at the start of the drivethrough.

Battle Maps

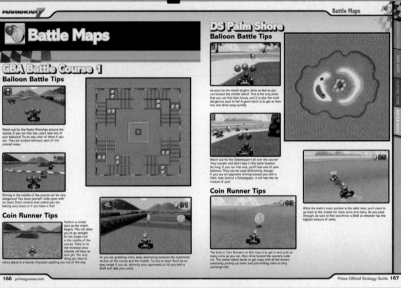

There's no way to predict what will happen in a battle, but these maps and tips can give you an edge over the competition.

Secret Checklists

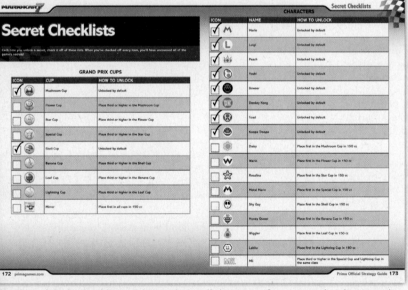

Use these handy checklists to learn about all the secret features and to keep track of each one you unlock.

TIP

Tip boxes usually indicate actions that might improve your performance, reveal a secret, or simply enhance your overall experience.

NOTE

Note boxes generally contain additional information without recommending a course of action.

CAUTION

Caution boxes aim to prevent costly mistakes. When you spot one of these boxes, make sure you read it!

Drivers Education

Game Modes

Mario Kart 7 offers a variety of single-player and multiplayer game modes. Select one of the available modes to test your karting skills on your own, with your friends, or against challengers from around the world!

Grand Prix

Select a Grand Prix cup to compete in a series of four races. Points are rewarded based on your position at the end of each race. At the end of the cup, the points are tallied to determine the winner. If you finish a cup in one of the top three slots, you receive a trophy to commemorate the event! You also receive a rating of zero to three stars, based on your overall performance. To improve your chances of a maximum rating, protect yourself from incoming attacks, avoid falling off of the track, and, of course, win every race in the cup!

Grand Prix events are available in three different classes and—eventually—Mirror Mode. Classes determine the power of the karts. 50cc is the slowest class, increasing with 100cc and 150cc. The class you choose also determines potential rewards, so consider participating in all of them.

At the start of a new game, most Grand Prix cups are locked. Place third or higher in an available cup to unlock the next one.

Collect coins in Grand Prix mode to unlock new kart parts. You can finish each race with a maximum of 10 coins—any coins you carry across the finish line are added to your current total. Each time you collect a predetermined number of coins, a random part becomes available.

NOTE

Characters and kart parts are discussed later in this guide. Read on to find out how to unlock them!

COINS

Coins also increase your kart's maximum speed. To get the most out of coins, try to collect them early in a race. You'll lose coins each time your kart spins out or falls over; replace lost coins as quickly as possible!

Time Trials

The Time Trials mode is all about speed. Pick the best kart, plan the best route, and find the best spot to use the three Mushrooms given to you at the start of each event. Your best performance is automatically saved as ghost data. If you wish, you can use available ghost data to re-create the recorded performance in your next Time Trial.

TIP

Reviewing ghost data is a great way to master a specific track. You can follow the ghost data and look for ways to improve on its performance or to test the effectiveness of alternate routes. Each time you fall behind the ghost data, try to determine exactly what caused it.

Balloon Battle

In Balloon Battle mode, your goal is to pop your opponents' balloons with the items scattered around the map. The player or team that pops the most balloons before the time expires wins the match. Each player starts the match with three balloons; if you lose all of your balloons, your current popped-balloon count is lowered.

Coin Runners

In the Coin Runners mode, you're tasked with collecting the coins scattered around the map. Victory is awarded to the player or team holding the most coins at the match. Each time you're knocked over or suffer a spinout, you lose some of your coins.

Multiplayer

The VS mode, Balloon Battle, and Coin Runners modes are also available for online multiplayer competition. If you play using local wireless you will have access to Grand Prix, Balloon Battle, and Coin Runners. Consult the game manual for details on joining or hosting a multiplayer game.

Worldwide

Select the Worldwide mode to challenge players from all over the world to race and battle in online matches. Your performance in the Worldwide game mode determines your VS Rating.

VS RATING

Your VS Rating (VR) is determined by your performance in Worldwide matches. You start out with a VR of 1,000 points. As you win or lose matches, you'll gain and lose VR points accordingly. Each time you start a new ranked match, you'll be grouped with opponents with comparable VS Ratings.

Additional Features
Street Pass

This feature allows you to exchange Mii characters and ghost data with other players.

Spot Pass

The Spot Pass feature automatically downloads ghost data and community recommendations from players around the world.

Controlling Your Kart

Before you hit the track, learn how to control your kart.

BASIC CONTROLS

ACTION	COMMAND
Accelerate	Press and hold Ⓨ or Ⓐ
Brake/Reverse	Press and hold Ⓑ
Steer	Push the Circle Pad left/right
Hop	Tap Ⓡ
Use item	Ⓛ or Ⓧ

FIRST-PERSON CAMERA

Press ✚ to switch to the first-person camera. While this view is active, you can steer your cart by tilting your Nintendo 3DS system from side to side. Press ✚, ✚, or ✚ to switch back to the normal camera.

TIP

If you prefer to race in first person view without use of the gyro sensor, head into the Mario Kart Channel and go into the Settings to turn it off.

Advanced Techniques

The basic controls will take you only so far. Master these advanced techniques to become a real competitor!

Rocket Start

Rev your engine at just the right time to boost off the starting line! To perform a rocket start, hold down Ⓨ or Ⓐ an instant after the countdown reaches 2.

Drift

Drifting allows you to take turns at much higher speeds than would otherwise be possible. When you start a turn, press and hold Ⓡ. After the hop, your kart will begin to drift. Use the Circle Pad to adjust the angle of your drift. Release Ⓡ to end your drift.

Mini-Turbo

Maintain a drift until blue sparks shoot from your kart's tires. At this point, release Ⓡ to perform a Mini-Turbo. Mini-Turbos provide a short speed boost.

Super Mini-Turbo

If you maintain a drift long enough, the blue sparks eventually turn orange. Release Ⓡ at this time to perform a Super Mini-Turbo. A Super Mini-Turbo provides a larger speed boost than a Mini-Turbo.

TIP

A number of factors determine the amount of time it takes to charge a Mini-Turbo or Super Mini-Turbo, but the angle of your drift is one of the most important elements. The harder your drift, the faster you build up a speed boost!

Jump Boost

Press Ⓡ to hop as you jump from an inclined surface. If you time it properly, you gain a short speed boost when you land.

Spin Turn

When moving forward isn't an option, use a spin turn to get back on track. While your kart is stopped, hold down Ⓐ (or Ⓨ) and Ⓑ at the same time, then push the Circle Pad to the left or right to turn on the spot.

Drafting

Drafting can be tough to pull off, but a successful attempt provides a significant speed boost. To use this technique, you must drive directly behind another racer. After a moment, air currents start zipping around you; this is the first stage of drafting. Stay behind your opponent until your kart shoots forward with a burst of speed.

JOSTLING

Jostling isn't exactly an advanced technique, but it's certainly an important one. To jostle, simply steer your kart into another racer. Use this technique to knock an opponent away from item boxes or into obstacles. Heavy racers excel at jostling, but with enough speed, even the smallest racers can bully their opponents with a well-aimed jostle.

Using Terrain

Most courses contain a wide variety of terrain, and your kart performs differently on each of them. Consider the basic properties of each terrain type when you evaluate alternate routes and potential shortcuts.

Land

Tracks can be composed of anything from tree branches to rainbows! When it comes to classifying terrain, however, the main road or path along each course is considered "land." Land comes in a variety of textures and colors, but it always provides adequate surface for high-speed karting.

Off-Road

If you head off-road, you'll generally notice a sharp decline in your kart's performance. Off-road surfaces like grass, sand, and snow can slow you down dramatically. Some karts can handle the loss of traction better than others, but none of them are at their best when driving off-road. When an off-road shortcut is too tempting to pass up, use an item to boost across unfavorable terrain.

Water

Your kart can achieve reasonable speeds in the water, but you'll definitely notice the difference in performance. Drifts are less effective through underwater turns, but they're the best way to maintain your speed.

Air

Your kart's glider deploys only under special circumstances, but you'll enjoy some excellent benefits when it does. After the initial speed boost, you can soar over obstacles and rough terrain until you glide back down to the ground.

DASH PANELS

Drive across a dash panel to receive a significant speed boost. The most common dash panels are predominantly orange. Drive across one of these dash panels to speed along the ground. When you drive across a glide panel, your kart deploys its glider, and the boost lifts you into the air. Glide panels are usually located on ramps or other inclined surfaces, allowing you to reach some truly impressive heights.

Items

Using Items

Item Box

During competitive events, you'll find item boxes located throughout the course. To collect an item, simply drive through an item box! The reward you receive is somewhat random, but your current position in the race has a large effect on the outcome. When you're doing well, you're much more likely to receive common items like Bananas and Shells. When you're doing poorly, you can expect more powerful items such as Lightning and Super Stars.

Items can have a dramatic effect on a race, so it's important to grab as many as possible. Determining the right time to use an item isn't easy, but you'll almost always want to do so before you reach the next item box!

Equipping Items

If an item can be equipped, press Ⓛ or Ⓧ. Depending on the item, you may need to hold Ⓛ or Ⓧ to keep it equipped. Equipping items can have various effects, but it generally results in some form of protection. Items like Bananas and Shells can be used to block most projectiles. This tactic brings versatility to seemingly straightforward items. Should you cling to the protection an equipped item affords, or use it as an offensive weapon and make a push for the lead? The answer, of course, is different for every racer and every situation.

If nearby opponents are well armed, you may want to hang on to that item a bit longer than you otherwise would have. On the other hand, if you find an opportunity to lay a Banana around a blind corner, ricochet a Green Shell through a narrow passage, or pick off a leading racer with a Red Shell, the risk could be outweighed by the potential rewards.

Throwing Items

After you equip an item, press Ⓛ or Ⓧ to throw it. If you must hold Ⓛ or Ⓧ to keep the item equipped, simply release Ⓛ or Ⓧ to throw it. Before a throw, press and hold up or down on the Circle Pad, then press Ⓛ or Ⓧ to toss the item in the corresponding direction.

NOTE

Different items have different trajectories and effects when thrown. Consider the unique properties of your equipped item before you commit to throwing it.

Equipable Items

Most of these items can be used for both offensive and defensive purposes. Learn the specifics of each equipable item to find an edge in almost any situation!

Banana

When a kart runs over a Banana, it spins out. Hold Ⓛ or Ⓧ to equip a Banana, then release Ⓛ or Ⓧ to drop it. To throw a Banana ahead of you, press and hold up on the Circle Pad before you release Ⓛ or Ⓧ. Bananas are most effective when you place them along narrow paths.

Triple Bananas

Triple Bananas are among the most versatile items in the game. Press Ⓛ or Ⓧ to drag three Bananas behind your kart. Press Ⓛ or Ⓧ to drop one of your Bananas behind you. Press and hold up on the Circle Pad, then press Ⓛ or Ⓧ to throw it ahead of you.

Since you don't have to hold Ⓛ or Ⓧ to keep Triple Bananas equipped, this item is one of your most convenient defensive options. Swerve in front of encroaching enemies to keep them at bay, or simply use them as you would a single Banana.

Green Shell

Green Shells knock over the first kart they hit. These projectiles travel in a straight line, but they'll change direction if they bounce off a suitable object. Hold Ⓛ or Ⓧ to equip a Green Shell, then release Ⓛ or Ⓧ to throw it ahead of you. To throw it behind you, press and hold down on the Circle Pad before you release Ⓛ or Ⓧ. This is an excellent option when you find yourself drifting through a narrow passage. As the Shell bounces off the walls, it makes a formidable obstacle for trailing racers.

Triple Green Shells

To equip Triple Green Shells, press Ⓛ or Ⓧ. As the shells circle your cart, press Ⓛ or Ⓧ to use one. As with a standard Green Shell, you can use the Circle Pad to aim the throw behind you.

While equipped, Triple Green Shells provide exceptional protection from incoming attacks. Veer into nearby racers to knock them over, or throw your shells to attack from a distance. Don't act without considering your options; each time you use (or lose) a Shell, you become more vulnerable to attacks.

Red Shell

Red Shells lock onto the closest kart in front of you. Press
ⓛ or ⓧ to equip a Red Shell, then release ⓛ or ⓧ to throw
it. These speedy projectiles are extremely hard to dodge, but
they're easily thwarted by equipped items. On a successful
hit, however, a Red Shell flips its target over.

To aim a Red Shell behind you, press and hold down on the
Circle Pad before you throw it. Keep in mind that when you
do this, the Red Shell loses its homing ability!

Triple Red Shells

Tap ⓛ or ⓧ to equip the shells, then press ⓛ or ⓧ each
time you wish to use one. This item offers all of the tactical
options of Triple Green Shells, with the added benefit of the
Red Shell's homing ability!

Bob-omb

This powerful explosive means big trouble for any kart
unfortunate enough get caught in the blast. Hold ⓛ or ⓧ to
equip a Bob-omb, then release ⓛ or ⓧ to throw it. To drop
the Bob-omb behind you, press and hold down on the Circle
Pad before you throw it.

Lucky 7

When equipped, the Lucky 7 surrounds your kart with seven
items! Press ⓛ or ⓧ to equip it, then press ⓛ or ⓧ again
to use one of the items. To select a specific item, press ⓛ
or ⓧ as it moves in front of you. Each Lucky 7 contains the
following items:

- Banana
- Green Shell
- Red Shell
- Bob-omb
- Super Star
- Mushroom
- Blooper

If you're flipped over while the Lucky 7 is equipped, you'll
lose all of your remaining items—beware of incoming
attacks!

TIP

When you're fortunate enough to get a Lucky 7, consider using the Bob-omb first. Ditching this explosive item minimizes
the chance you'll be caught in the blast. If an opponent
crashes into the Bob-omb while its equipped, you'll lose the
rest of your items.

Tactical Items

Once activated, these items last for only a short time. They may lack the versatility of equipable items, but they are invaluable in bad situations. To make the most of tactical items, you must choose the right moment to activate them.

Spiny Shell

Spiny Shells seek out the leading kart and knock it over on impact. Racers inside of the blast will suffer the same fate, as will any racers careless enough to drive in the Spiny Shell's path. Press L or Ⓧ to throw a Spiny Shell.

Spiny Shells are absolutely relentless. If an opponent throws one of these while you're in the lead, you'd better brace yourself for its arrival; unless you get your hands on a Super Star, this item is virtually guaranteed to catch you.

Triple Mushrooms

Press L or Ⓧ each time you want to use one of these Mushrooms for a short speed boost. You can gain a lot of ground with Triple Mushrooms!

Golden Mushroom

The Golden Mushroom provides a speed boost each time you press L or Ⓧ. However, this effect doesn't last long; once you use a Golden Mushroom, boost repeatedly until it expires.

Mushroom

Press L or Ⓧ to use a Mushroom for a short speed boost. Mushrooms are best used to cut across rough terrain or to recover from collisions.

INTRODUCTION
NEW CUPS
CLASSIC CUPS
BATTLE MAPS

Bullet Bill

The Bullet Bill item temporarily transforms you into a Bullet Bill. Press ⓛ or Ⓧ to use this item. While the transformation is active, you automatically follow the course at much higher speeds that you could normally drive. As an added bonus, the Bullet Bill knocks over any karts along its path!

Blooper

Soon after you press ⓛ or Ⓧ to use a Blooper, it sprays ink on all of the karts ahead of you. The ink impairs the vision of all affected drivers. This item is best used when leading opponents are negotiating treacherous turns or roaming hazards. If you find yourself covered in ink, try to recall nearby dangers, and slow down as needed.

INTRDOUCTION

NEW CUPS

CLASSIC CUPS

BATTLE MAPS

Lightning

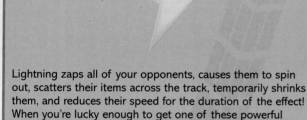

Lightning zaps all of your opponents, causes them to spin out, scatters their items across the track, temporarily shrinks them, and reduces their speed for the duration of the effect! When you're lucky enough to get one of these powerful items, press ⒧ or Ⓧ to use it. Lightning is most effective when leading opponents are drifting near unfenced turns or gliding over unsafe terrain.

Fire Flower

While active, this item allows you to throw fireballs! The fireballs have a limited range, but you can use them to attack several opponents with a single item. Any kart struck by a fireball spins out of control.

Press ⒧ or Ⓧ to use a Fire Flower, then repeatedly tap ⒧ or Ⓧ to make additional attacks. To throw fireballs behind you, hold down on the Circle Pad while you press ⒧ or Ⓧ .

Super Star

The Super Star grants temporary invincibility. While the effect is active, you're immune to all incoming attacks, your top speed is increased, and you'll knock over any karts you hit!

After you collect a Super Star, press ⒧ or Ⓧ to use it.

Super Leaf

When you press ⒧ or Ⓧ to activate a Super Leaf, a tail is placed on your kart. Press ⒧ or Ⓧ to swing the tail at nearby racers or to swat away objects such as Shells and Bananas. The Super Leaf lasts only a short time, but you'll lose it instantly if you fail to deflect an incoming item.

Characters

The character you select affects various aspects of your kart. From its top speed to the way it handles terrain, it all starts with the driver. Not all characters are available when you start a new game, but as you progress through the Grand Prix cups, you'll gain access to more of them. If you spot a character you're eager to try out, look for the conditions required to unlock them!

Many of the characters share similar statistics, but you'll find enough variety to test every aspect of racing. Remember that your kart assembly can enhance or offset any of the driver's characteristics. If you have your heart set on a particular character, you can always build a kart around them!

Default Characters

These characters are unlocked and ready to race! This group contains a nice selection of character types, so you shouldn't have any trouble finding one that matches your style of play.

Mario

With his well-rounded characteristics, Mario sets the standard for kart racers!

WEIGHT

SPEED (LAND)

SPEED (SEA)

SPEED (SKY)

ACCELERATION

HANDLING (LAND)

HANDLING (SEA)

HANDLING (SKY)

OFF-ROADING

MINI-TURBO

STABILITY

DRIFT

Luigi

Luigi shares the same basic qualities as his brother, making him a great choice for all players.

WEIGHT

SPEED (LAND)

SPEED (SEA)

SPEED (SKY)

ACCELERATION

HANDLING (LAND)

HANDLING (SEA)

HANDLING (SKY)

OFF-ROADING

MINI-TURBO

STABILITY

DRIFT

Peach

Peach's top speed is a bit slower than heavier racers, but she gives a nice boost to your kart's acceleration.

WEIGHT	HANDLING (SEA)
SPEED (LAND)	HANDLING (SKY)
SPEED (SEA)	OFF-ROADING
SPEED (SKY)	MINI-TURBO
ACCELERATION	STABILITY
HANDLING (LAND)	DRIFT

Peach

Yoshi

Like Peach, Yoshi favors acceleration over top speed. He's slightly bigger than a true lightweight, but not by much!

WEIGHT	HANDLING (SEA)
SPEED (LAND)	HANDLING (SKY)
SPEED (SEA)	OFF-ROADING
SPEED (SKY)	MINI-TURBO
ACCELERATION	STABILITY
HANDLING (LAND)	DRIFT

Yoshi

Bowser

This heavy hitter has a high top speed and enough weight to jostle through almost anyone. Unfortunately for Bowser, these attributes come at the cost of acceleration, handling, and nearly every other kart characteristic.

WEIGHT	HANDLING (SEA)
SPEED (LAND)	HANDLING (SKY)
SPEED (SEA)	OFF-ROADING
SPEED (SKY)	MINI-TURBO
ACCELERATION	STABILITY
HANDLING (LAND)	DRIFT

Bowser

Donkey Kong

Donkey Kong may not be able to match Bowser's weight and speed, but he makes up for it with improved acceleration. If you're not ready to try a true heavyweight, consider giving Donkey Kong a spin.

WEIGHT	HANDLING (SEA)
SPEED (LAND)	HANDLING (SKY)
SPEED (SEA)	OFF-ROADING
SPEED (SKY)	MINI-TURBO
ACCELERATION	STABILITY
HANDLING (LAND)	DRIFT

Donkey Kong

Toad

Toad's lack of weight and speed is offset by his outstanding acceleration and drifting ability. Lightweight characters are great for new players, and Toad is one of the best around!

WEIGHT	HANDLING (SEA)
SPEED (LAND)	HANDLING (SKY)
SPEED (SEA)	OFF-ROADING
SPEED (SKY)	MINI-TURBO
ACCELERATION	STABILITY
HANDLING (LAND)	DRIFT

Toad

Koopa Troopa

This little guy is another great option for new players. He shares all of Toad's characteristics, so don't hesitate to pick him.

WEIGHT	HANDLING (SEA)
SPEED (LAND)	HANDLING (SKY)
SPEED (SEA)	OFF-ROADING
SPEED (SKY)	MINI-TURBO
ACCELERATION	STABILITY
HANDLING (LAND)	DRIFT

Koopa Troopa

Secret Characters

The secret is out! If you perform well enough in the Grand Prix cups, you'll be rewarded with these characters. You'll see some familiar faces here, but this group also contains some exciting new additions!

Daisy

Daisy wasn't about to sit by while her friends had all the fun. Like Peach and Yoshi, Daisy balances relatively low speed with great acceleration.

WEIGHT

SPEED (LAND)

SPEED (SEA)

SPEED (SKY)

ACCELERATION

HANDLING (LAND)

HANDLING (SEA)

HANDLING (SKY)

OFF-ROADING

MINI-TURBO

STABILITY

DRIFT

To unlock Daisy, take first place in the 150 cc Mushroom Cup.

Wario

Wario is back to show these racers how things are done. Like Bowser, Wario is a true heavyweight. He can reach high speeds, and he's great at jostling, but his other characteristics are somewhat lacking.

WEIGHT

SPEED (LAND)

SPEED (SEA)

SPEED (SKY)

ACCELERATION

HANDLING (LAND)

HANDLING (SEA)

HANDLING (SKY)

OFF-ROADING

MINI-TURBO

STABILITY

DRIFT

To unlock Wario, take first place in the 150 cc Flower Cup.

INTRODUCTION

NEW CUPS

CLASSIC CUPS

BATTLE MAPS

Rosalina

Rosalina may not look it, but she has the same characteristics as Donkey Kong! Of course, one would expect the protector of the cosmos could hold her own. Rosalina is another great option for players who want to put a little more muscle into their jostling.

WEIGHT	HANDLING (SEA)
SPEED (LAND)	HANDLING (SKY)
SPEED (SEA)	OFF-ROADING
SPEED (SKY)	MINI-TURBO
ACCELERATION	STABILITY
HANDLING (LAND)	DRIFT

Rosalina

To unlock Rosalina, take first place in the 150 cc Star Cup.

Metal Mario

You'll find larger racers on the track, but you won't find anyone tougher. Metal Mario is another true heavyweight, which means he's traded handling and acceleration for high speed and a powerful jostle.

WEIGHT	HANDLING (SEA)
SPEED (LAND)	HANDLING (SKY)
SPEED (SEA)	OFF-ROADING
SPEED (SKY)	MINI-TURBO
ACCELERATION	STABILITY
HANDLING (LAND)	DRIFT

Metal Mario

To unlock Metal Mario, take first place in the 150 cc Special Cup.

Shy Guy

This plucky lightweight has the outstanding acceleration and drifting you'd expect from someone his size. Like similar characters, his speed is fairly low, but Shy Guy has nothing to be ashamed of.

WEIGHT

SPEED (LAND)

SPEED (SEA)

SPEED (SKY)

ACCELERATION

HANDLING (LAND)

HANDLING (SEA)

HANDLING (SKY)

OFF-ROADING

MINI-TURBO

STABILITY

DRIFT

Shy Guy

To unlock Shy Guy, take first place in the 150 cc Shell Cup.

Honey Queen

Honey Queen is stepping out of the hive to try her hand at kart racing. She's not looking for trouble, but she has no reason to shy away from it. Honey Queen has all of the characteristics of a true heavyweight. She can reach high speeds, but it takes a while to do so.

WEIGHT

SPEED (LAND)

SPEED (SEA)

SPEED (SKY)

ACCELERATION

HANDLING (LAND)

HANDLING (SEA)

HANDLING (SKY)

OFF-ROADING

MINI-TURBO

STABILITY

DRIFT

Honey Queen

To unlock Honey Queen, take first place in the 150 cc Banana Cup.

Wiggler

Wiggler shares the characteristics of lighter heavyweights like Donkey Kong and Rosalina. This racer has a short fuse, so try not to fall behind!

WEIGHT	HANDLING (SEA)

SPEED (LAND)	HANDLING (SKY)

SPEED (SEA)	OFF-ROADING

SPEED (SKY)	MINI-TURBO

ACCELERATION	STABILITY

HANDLING (LAND)	DRIFT

Wiggler

To unlock Wiggler, take first place in the 150 cc Leaf Cup.

Lakitu

Lakitu got tired of officiating races, so he decided to enter one himself. Select this little guy to enjoy the acceleration and drifting shared by all lightweights.

WEIGHT	HANDLING (SEA)
SPEED (LAND)	HANDLING (SKY)
SPEED (SEA)	OFF-ROADING
SPEED (SKY)	MINI-TURBO
ACCELERATION	STABILITY
HANDLING (LAND)	DRIFT

Lakitu

To unlock Lakitu, take first place in the 150 cc Lightning Cup.

UNLOCKING YOUR MII

Earn the ability to race as your Mii. Finish in third place or higher in the Special Cup and Lightning Cup within the same class. Once you do, your newly available Mii appears on the selection screen.

Kart Assembly

Assembling your kart does more than show off your sense of style; your selections help determine its final characteristics. After you select a driver, choose a kart and then add tires and a glider to create your ideal racer.

From the nimble Egg 1 to the sleek B Dasher, there's something to satisfy everyone—as long as you've unlocked the parts. When you start a game, you have a few basic options. To unlock all of the secret parts, you'll have to test your skills in the Grand Prix cups. When playing alone, collect the coins from each track. Each time you collect enough to earn a reward, a random part is unlocked. Next time you assemble a kart, unwrap the gift box to see what you received.

There's no telling which part you'll get, but if you keep track of your coins, you'll always know when to expect your next reward:

UNLOCKING KART PARTS

SECRET PART	REQUIRED COINS	SECRET PART	REQUIRED COINS
Part 1	50	Part 13	1,000
Part 2	100	Part 14	1,200
Part 3	150	Part 15	1,400
Part 4	200	Part 16	1,600
Part 5	250	Part 17	1,800
Part 6	300	Part 18	2,000
Part 7	400	Part 19	2,500
Part 8	500	Part 20	3,000
Part 9	600	Part 21	3,500
Part 10	700	Part 22	4,000
Part 11	800	Part 23	4,500
Part 12	900	Part 24	5,000

During online play, you have an alternate way to unlock kart parts. If you claim victory over a Mii user who is connected to StreetPass, you can obtain one of the parts that player was using! No matter your chosen method, try to collect every part. The more options you have at your disposal, the better your chances of assembling a kart that complements your play style!

NOTE

The coins collected in Multiplayer Grand Prix and VS Mode also count toward unlocks.

GOLD PARTS

Unlike most kart parts, gold parts are not unlocked at random. Each gold part has two specific conditions attached to it; meet at least one of these conditions to unlock the part. For specific details, look for the gold parts at the end of each list.

Be warned! Gold parts indicate a significant achievement. You'll have to put in a lot of time to earn one.

TIP

Each kart part has several secret characteristics. Use this section to learn the hidden details of each part. Make an informed choice!

Your choice of kart effects almost all aspects of the final assembly, but there are a few characteristics that vary greatly from kart to kart—not all of which are indicated during kart assembly. When comparing karts, note the dramatic differences between land speed, water speed, and Mini-Turbo characteristics.

Karts

Default Karts

These karts are available at the start of a new game.

Standard

WEIGHT	HANDLING (SEA)
SPEED (LAND)	HANDLING (SKY)
SPEED (SEA)	OFF-ROADING
SPEED (SKY)	MINI-TURBO
ACCELERATION	STABILITY
HANDLING (LAND)	DRIFT

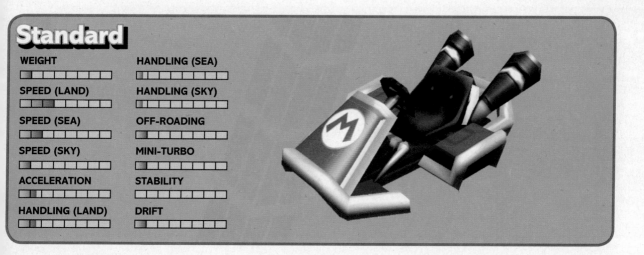

Bolt Buggy

WEIGHT	HANDLING (SEA)
SPEED (LAND)	HANDLING (SKY)
SPEED (SEA)	OFF-ROADING
SPEED (SKY)	MINI-TURBO
ACCELERATION	STABILITY
HANDLING (LAND)	DRIFT

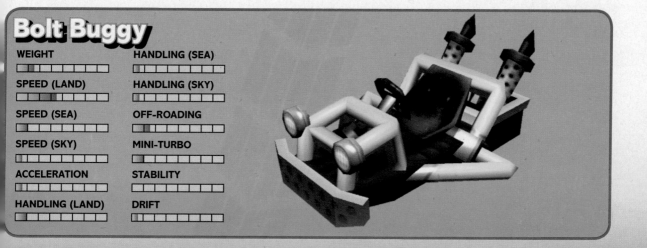

INTRDOUCTION
NEW CUPS
CLASSIC CUPS
BATTLE MAPS

Birthday Girl

WEIGHT	**HANDLING (SEA)**
SPEED (LAND)	**HANDLING (SKY)**
SPEED (SEA)	**OFF-ROADING**
SPEED (SKY)	**MINI-TURBO**
ACCELERATION	**STABILITY**
HANDLING (LAND)	**DRIFT**

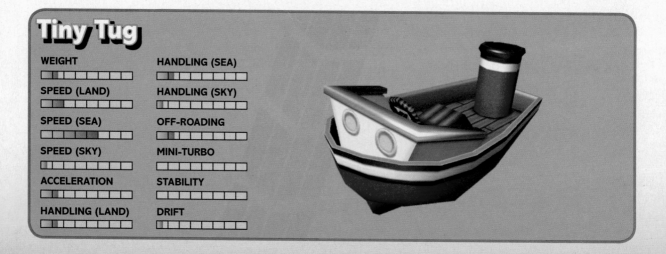

Secret Karts

As you collect coins in Grand Prix, these karts are unlocked in random order.

Egg 1

WEIGHT	**HANDLING (SEA)**
SPEED (LAND)	**HANDLING (SKY)**
SPEED (SEA)	**OFF-ROADING**
SPEED (SKY)	**MINI-TURBO**
ACCELERATION	**STABILITY**
HANDLING (LAND)	**DRIFT**

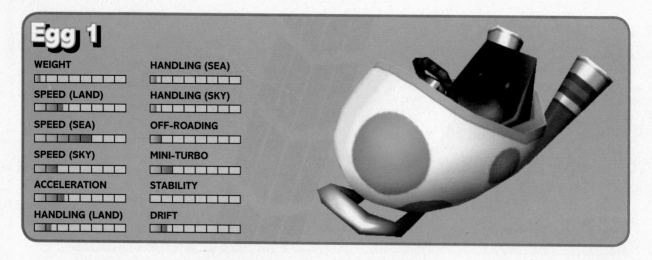

Tiny Tug

WEIGHT	**HANDLING (SEA)**
SPEED (LAND)	**HANDLING (SKY)**
SPEED (SEA)	**OFF-ROADING**
SPEED (SKY)	**MINI-TURBO**
ACCELERATION	**STABILITY**
HANDLING (LAND)	**DRIFT**

Cloud 9

WEIGHT	HANDLING (SEA)
SPEED (LAND)	HANDLING (SKY)
SPEED (SEA)	OFF-ROADING
SPEED (SKY)	MINI-TURBO
ACCELERATION	STABILITY
HANDLING (LAND)	DRIFT

Zucchini

WEIGHT	HANDLING (SEA)
SPEED (LAND)	HANDLING (SKY)
SPEED (SEA)	OFF-ROADING
SPEED (SKY)	MINI-TURBO
ACCELERATION	STABILITY
HANDLING (LAND)	DRIFT

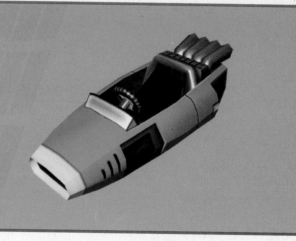

B Dasher

WEIGHT	HANDLING (SEA)
SPEED (LAND)	HANDLING (SKY)
SPEED (SEA)	OFF-ROADING
SPEED (SKY)	MINI-TURBO
ACCELERATION	STABILITY
HANDLING (LAND)	DRIFT

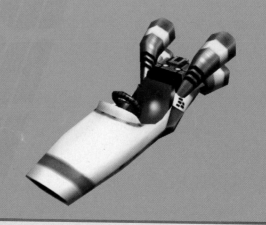

Bruiser

WEIGHT	**HANDLING (SEA)**
SPEED (LAND)	**HANDLING (SKY)**
SPEED (SEA)	**OFF-ROADING**
SPEED (SKY)	**MINI-TURBO**
ACCELERATION	**STABILITY**
HANDLING (LAND)	**DRIFT**

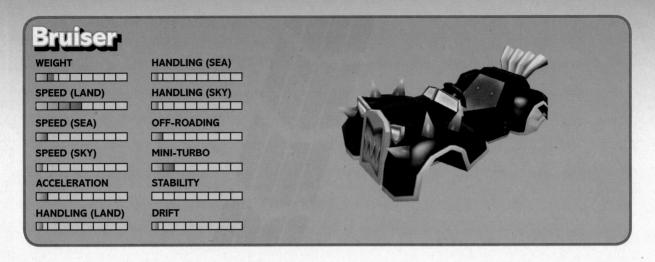

Bumble V

WEIGHT	**HANDLING (SEA)**
SPEED (LAND)	**HANDLING (SKY)**
SPEED (SEA)	**OFF-ROADING**
SPEED (SKY)	**MINI-TURBO**
ACCELERATION	**STABILITY**
HANDLING (LAND)	**DRIFT**

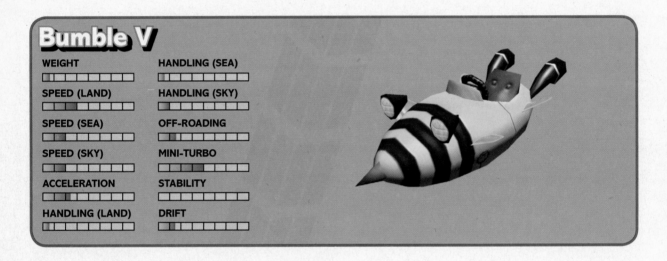

Koopa Clown

WEIGHT	**HANDLING (SEA)**
SPEED (LAND)	**HANDLING (SKY)**
SPEED (SEA)	**OFF-ROADING**
SPEED (SKY)	**MINI-TURBO**
ACCELERATION	**STABILITY**
HANDLING (LAND)	**DRIFT**

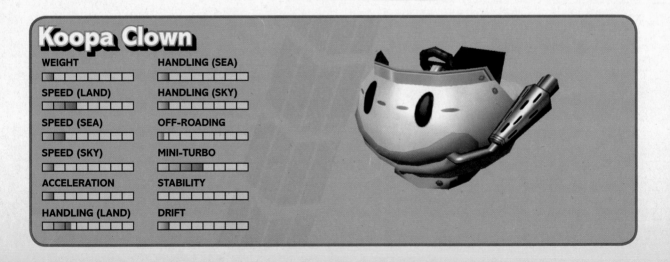

Pipe Frame

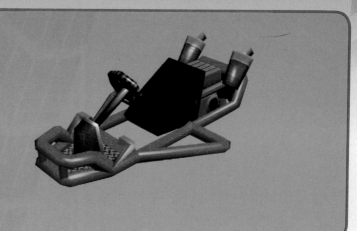

WEIGHT

SPEED (LAND)

SPEED (SEA)

SPEED (SKY)

ACCELERATION

HANDLING (LAND)

HANDLING (SEA)

HANDLING (SKY)

OFF-ROADING

MINI-TURBO

STABILITY

DRIFT

Blue Seven

WEIGHT

SPEED (LAND)

SPEED (SEA)

SPEED (SKY)

ACCELERATION

HANDLING (LAND)

HANDLING (SEA)

HANDLING (SKY)

OFF-ROADING

MINI-TURBO

STABILITY

DRIFT

Cact-X

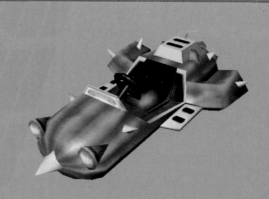

WEIGHT

SPEED (LAND)

SPEED (SEA)

SPEED (SKY)

ACCELERATION

HANDLING (LAND)

HANDLING (SEA)

HANDLING (SKY)

OFF-ROADING

MINI-TURBO

STABILITY

DRIFT

Barrel Train

WEIGHT	**HANDLING (SEA)**
SPEED (LAND)	**HANDLING (SKY)**
SPEED (SEA)	**OFF-ROADING**
SPEED (SKY)	**MINI-TURBO**
ACCELERATION	**STABILITY**
HANDLING (LAND)	**DRIFT**

Soda Jet

WEIGHT	**HANDLING (SEA)**
SPEED (LAND)	**HANDLING (SKY)**
SPEED (SEA)	**OFF-ROADING**
SPEED (SKY)	**MINI-TURBO**
ACCELERATION	**STABILITY**
HANDLING (LAND)	**DRIFT**

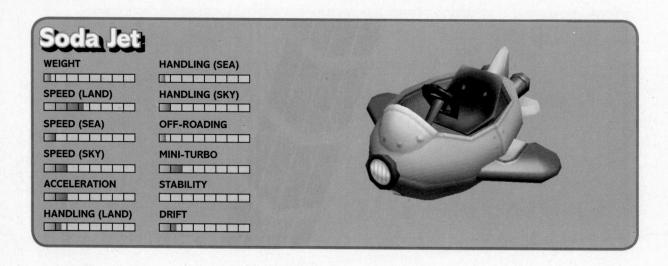

Gold Standard

WEIGHT	**HANDLING (SEA)**
SPEED (LAND)	**HANDLING (SKY)**
SPEED (SEA)	**OFF-ROADING**
SPEED (SKY)	**MINI-TURBO**
ACCELERATION	**STABILITY**
HANDLING (LAND)	**DRIFT**

To unlock the Gold Standard, obtain a VR higher than 10,000 points, or collect 20,000 coins from the Grand Prix cups.

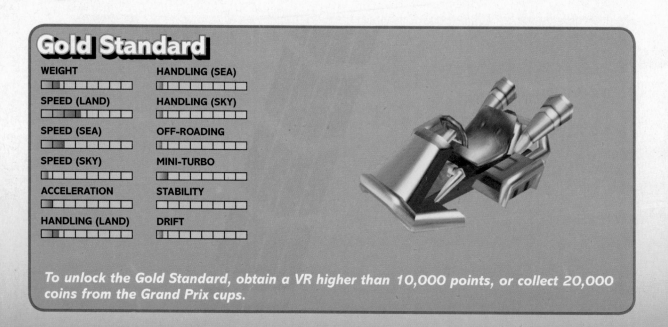

Tires

Tires affect several aspects of your final kart, but the most notable characteristics deal with speed and handling across various terrain types. It's also worth noting that tire selection is the only way to alter your kart's stability.

Default Tires

These tires are available at the start of a new game.

Standard

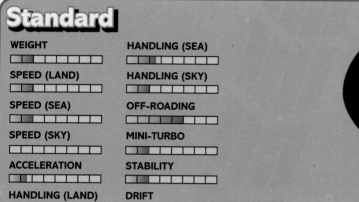

WEIGHT	HANDLING (SEA)
SPEED (LAND)	HANDLING (SKY)
SPEED (SEA)	OFF-ROADING
SPEED (SKY)	MINI-TURBO
ACCELERATION	STABILITY
HANDLING (LAND)	DRIFT

Monster

WEIGHT	HANDLING (SEA)
SPEED (LAND)	HANDLING (SKY)
SPEED (SEA)	OFF-ROADING
SPEED (SKY)	MINI-TURBO
ACCELERATION	STABILITY
HANDLING (LAND)	DRIFT

Roller

WEIGHT	HANDLING (SEA)
SPEED (LAND)	HANDLING (SKY)
SPEED (SEA)	OFF-ROADING
SPEED (SKY)	MINI-TURBO
ACCELERATION	STABILITY
HANDLING (LAND)	DRIFT

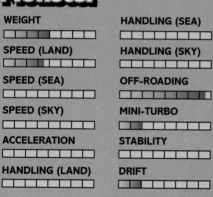

Secret Tires

As you collect coins in Grand Prix, you unlock these tires in random order.

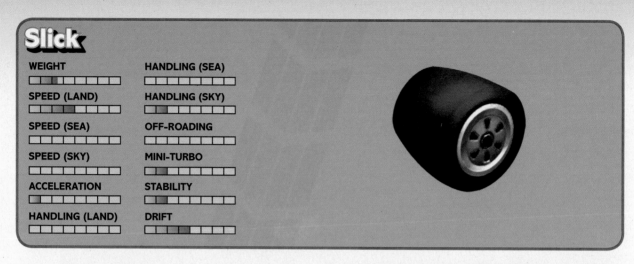

Slick

WEIGHT	HANDLING (SEA)
SPEED (LAND)	HANDLING (SKY)
SPEED (SEA)	OFF-ROADING
SPEED (SKY)	MINI-TURBO
ACCELERATION	STABILITY
HANDLING (LAND)	DRIFT

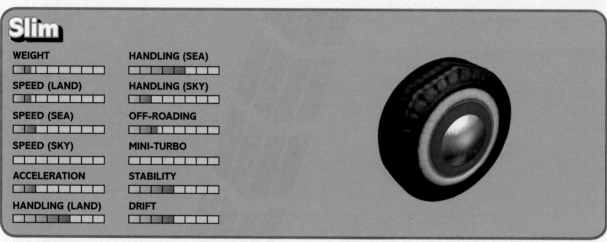

Slim

WEIGHT	HANDLING (SEA)
SPEED (LAND)	HANDLING (SKY)
SPEED (SEA)	OFF-ROADING
SPEED (SKY)	MINI-TURBO
ACCELERATION	STABILITY
HANDLING (LAND)	DRIFT

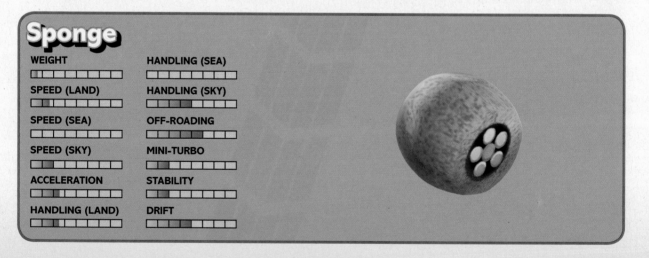

Sponge

WEIGHT	HANDLING (SEA)
SPEED (LAND)	HANDLING (SKY)
SPEED (SEA)	OFF-ROADING
SPEED (SKY)	MINI-TURBO
ACCELERATION	STABILITY
HANDLING (LAND)	DRIFT

INTRODUCTION

NEW CUPS

CLASSIC CUPS

BATTLE MAPS

Red Monster

WEIGHT	**HANDLING (SEA)**
SPEED (LAND)	**HANDLING (SKY)**
SPEED (SEA)	**OFF-ROADING**
SPEED (SKY)	**MINI-TURBO**
ACCELERATION	**STABILITY**
HANDLING (LAND)	**DRIFT**

Mushroom

WEIGHT	**HANDLING (SEA)**
SPEED (LAND)	**HANDLING (SKY)**
SPEED (SEA)	**OFF-ROADING**
SPEED (SKY)	**MINI-TURBO**
ACCELERATION	**STABILITY**
HANDLING (LAND)	**DRIFT**

Wood

WEIGHT	**HANDLING (SEA)**
SPEED (LAND)	**HANDLING (SKY)**
SPEED (SEA)	**OFF-ROADING**
SPEED (SKY)	**MINI-TURBO**
ACCELERATION	**STABILITY**
HANDLING (LAND)	**DRIFT**

Gold Tires

WEIGHT	**HANDLING (SEA)**
SPEED (LAND)	**HANDLING (SKY)**
SPEED (SEA)	**OFF-ROADING**
SPEED (SKY)	**MINI-TURBO**
ACCELERATION	**STABILITY**
HANDLING (LAND)	**DRIFT**

To unlock the Gold Tires, obtain a minimum one-star rating in each cup of every class, or collect 15,000 coins from the Grand Prix cups.

Gliders

Gliders mainly affect your kart's speed and handling while in the air, but some gliders affect characteristics like acceleration and drifting.

Default Gliders

Only one glider is available at the start of a new game.

Super Glider

WEIGHT	**HANDLING (SEA)**
SPEED (LAND)	**HANDLING (SKY)**
SPEED (SEA)	**OFF-ROADING**
SPEED (SKY)	**MINI-TURBO**
ACCELERATION	**STABILITY**
HANDLING (LAND)	**DRIFT**

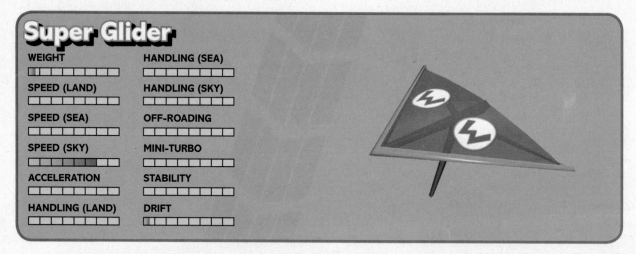

Secret Gliders

As you collect coins in Grand Prix, these gliders are unlocked in random order.

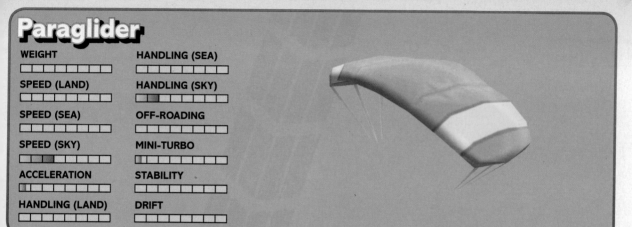

Paraglider

WEIGHT	HANDLING (SEA)
SPEED (LAND)	HANDLING (SKY)
SPEED (SEA)	OFF-ROADING
SPEED (SKY)	MINI-TURBO
ACCELERATION	STABILITY
HANDLING (LAND)	DRIFT

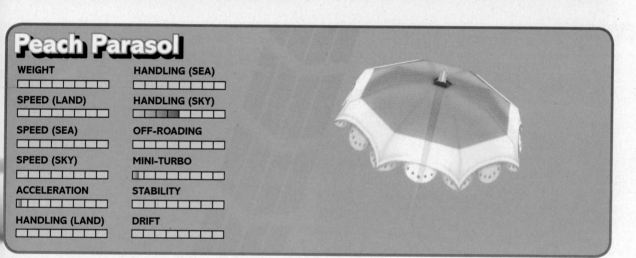

Peach Parasol

WEIGHT	HANDLING (SEA)
SPEED (LAND)	HANDLING (SKY)
SPEED (SEA)	OFF-ROADING
SPEED (SKY)	MINI-TURBO
ACCELERATION	STABILITY
HANDLING (LAND)	DRIFT

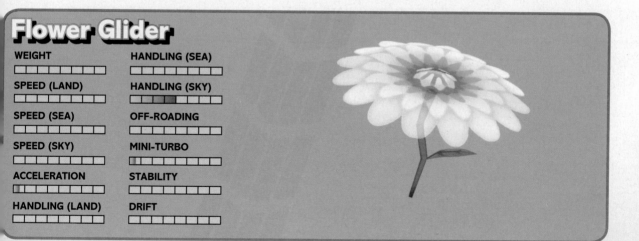

Flower Glider

WEIGHT	HANDLING (SEA)
SPEED (LAND)	HANDLING (SKY)
SPEED (SEA)	OFF-ROADING
SPEED (SKY)	MINI-TURBO
ACCELERATION	STABILITY
HANDLING (LAND)	DRIFT

Swooper

WEIGHT	**HANDLING (SEA)**
SPEED (LAND)	**HANDLING (SKY)**
SPEED (SEA)	**OFF-ROADING**
SPEED (SKY)	**MINI-TURBO**
ACCELERATION	**STABILITY**
HANDLING (LAND)	**DRIFT**

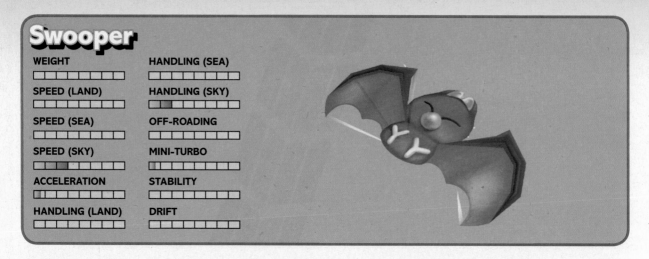

Beast Glider

WEIGHT	**HANDLING (SEA)**
SPEED (LAND)	**HANDLING (SKY)**
SPEED (SEA)	**OFF-ROADING**
SPEED (SKY)	**MINI-TURBO**
ACCELERATION	**STABILITY**
HANDLING (LAND)	**DRIFT**

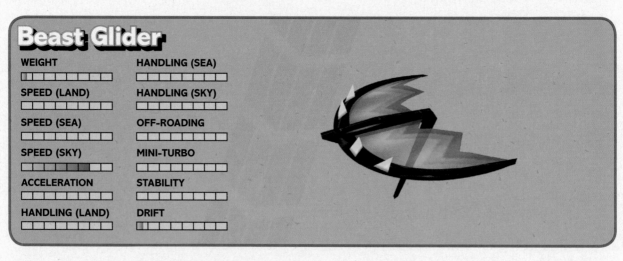

Gold Glider

WEIGHT	**HANDLING (SEA)**
SPEED (LAND)	**HANDLING (SKY)**
SPEED (SEA)	**OFF-ROADING**
SPEED (SKY)	**MINI-TURBO**
ACCELERATION	**STABILITY**
HANDLING (LAND)	**DRIFT**

To unlock the Gold Glider, connect to 100 people via StreetPass, or collect 10,000 coins from the Grand Prix cups.

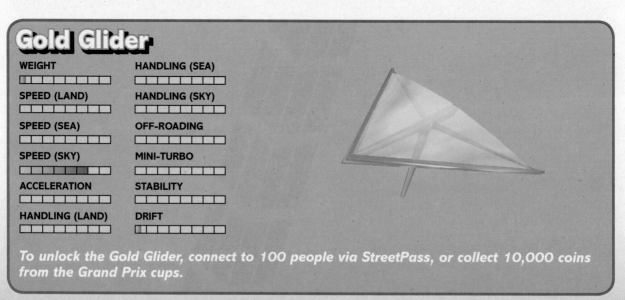

Drivethrough

Welcome to the Drivethrough! This section details proven strategies for all 32 courses. There's a lot of information to go through, but first let's have a look at how it's all organized.

Course Overview

These introductions list the cup name, the course name, and a brief description of the event.

Road Hazards

Here you'll find a summary of the course's most prominent threats, such as rough terrain, unfenced turns, and roaming enemies.

Time Trial

The first two pages of every course detail proven tactics to get you pure speed. Although these steps were intended for the various Time Trials, they're easily applied to the Grand Prix and multiplayer game modes. Each numbered step represents one or more suggested actions near the indicated location. When you read through this section, begin with step 1, then follow each step in order.

The Kart of Champions

Some of the world's best kart racers have competed for the top spots in the Time Trials courses. In this box, you'll see the character and kart combinations used by the best of the best. Keep in mind, each Kart of Champions box reflects the preferences of just one person. It's entirely possible for you to clock an even faster time with a kart of your own design.

We swapped out a few parts to improve our own efforts, and you should certainly do the same. Experiment with new characters and parts as you unlock them until you assemble your ideal kart!

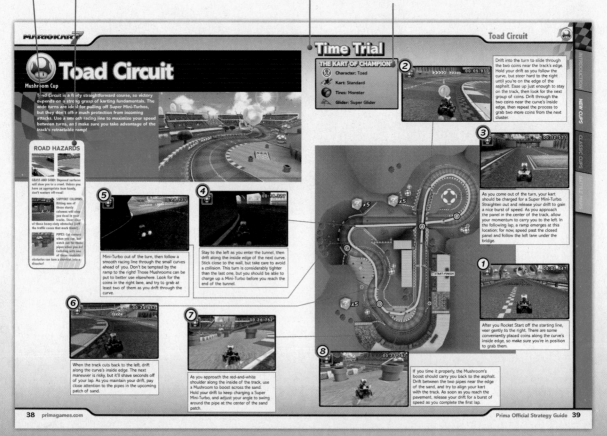

Grand Prix

Once you know the best way through a course, it's time to bring opponents into the mix. The Grand Prix section contains recommended tactics for combat situations. Each Grand Prix tactic is assigned a letter, and the relevant location is indicated by a corresponding letter on the course map. Since these tactics generally depend on variables like item availability and opponent actions, the Grand Prix section is less rigid than the Time Trial section. Review these tactics before a race, then react to what happens on the track.

Mirror Mode

We've provided a map for the Mirror mode version of each track. All of the established tactics work just as well in Mirror mode, but adjusting to the new turns can take some effort. Review this map to prepare for the challenge ahead of you.

MARIO KART 7 — Toad Circuit

TACTICS FOR LAPS 2 & 3

As you come out of the first curve of lap 2, look for the ramp at the track's center. Drive across the glide panel to soar over the bridge. Be sure to hop just before you take off to gain a little extra speed during your glide.

If needed, make small adjustments to your racing line to grab any conveniently located coins.

C 7th

The ramp toward the course's end offers a convenient shortcut—provided you have a Mushroom handy. As you exit the tunnel, veer to the right and approach the ramp head-on. Boost across the sand, then hop from the ramp's top to gain a little extra speed when you land.

Grand Prix

A 6th

You'll face some stiff competition for item boxes early in the race. As you approach the first curve, pay attention to the racers in front of you. If they're in position to clear out the item boxes, it's generally best to focus on the upcoming turn. As the pack thins out, you'll have a much easier time claiming items.

B 5th

As you come out of the first curve, check your opponents' karts for equipped items. You should gain some ground as you drift through the turn, but devious racers can keep you at bay with newly acquired items. As you head under the bridge, check the track for dropped items. If you have a Banana handy, try placing it just past one of the dash panels. If you don't see any immediate dangers, this straightaway is a great place to draft behind other racers.

D 8th

If you have an appropriate item, you can use the shortcut described in the "Time Trial" section. Before you venture onto the sand, check the Touch Screen for any dangerously armed opponents. An unanticipated attack can strand you off-road, making it very difficult to get back into the race. If you're not comfortable with the risk, you can still gain a lot of ground by cutting across the edge of the sand.

TIP

Your opponents will often avoid the coins along the track's outside edge; if you haven't collected 10 coins by your third lap, make a wide drift through the last curve to scoop up any remaining coins on your way to the finish line.

Mirror Mode

When you race this course in Mirror mode, use all of the same tactics described here—just do so in the opposite direction. Every left turn becomes a right one (and vice versa) when the course is flipped.

START/FINISH

INTRDOUCTION

NEW CUPS

CLASSIC CUPS

BATTLE MAPS

Toad Circuit

Mushroom Cup

Toad Circuit is a fairly straightforward course, so victory depends on a strong grasp of karting fundamentals. The wide turns are ideal for pulling off Super Mini-Turbos, but they don't offer much protection from incoming attacks. Use a smooth racing line to maximize your speed between turns, and make sure you take advantage of the track's retractable ramp!

ROAD HAZARDS

GRASS AND SAND: Unpaved surfaces will slow you to a crawl. Unless you have an appropriate item handy, don't venture off-road!

SUPPORT COLUMNS: Hitting one of these sturdy columns will stop you dead in your tracks. Steer clear of these heavy-duty obstacles (and the traffic cones that mark them!).

PIPES: Cut corners when you can, but watch out for these pipes when you do! Colliding with one of these roadside obstacles can turn a shortcut into a disaster!

5

Mini-Turbo out of the turn, then follow a smooth racing line through the small curves ahead of you. Don't be tempted by the ramp to the right! Those Mushrooms can be put to better use elsewhere. Look for the coins in the right lane, and try to grab at least two of them as you drift through the curve.

4

Stay to the left as you enter the tunnel, then drift along the inside edge of the next curve. Stick close to the wall, but take care to avoid a collision. This turn is considerably tighter than the last one, but you should be able to charge up a Mini-Turbo before you reach the end of the tunnel.

6

When the track cuts back to the left, drift along the curve's inside edge. The next maneuver is risky, but it'll shave seconds off of your lap. As you maintain your drift, pay close attention to the pipes in the upcoming patch of sand.

7

As you approach the red-and-white shoulder along the inside of the track, use a Mushroom to boost across the sand. Hold your drift to keep charging a Super Mini-Turbo, and adjust your angle to swing around the pipe at the center of the sand patch.

Time Trial

THE KART OF CHAMPIONS

 Character: Toad

 Kart: Standard

Tires: Monster

Glider: Super Glider

2 00:05.930

Drift into the turn to slide through the two coins near the track's edge. Hold your drift as you follow the curve, but steer hard to the right until you're on the edge of the asphalt. Ease up just enough to stay on the track, then look for the next group of coins. Drift through the two coins near the curve's inside edge, then repeat the process to grab two more coins from the next cluster.

3 00:12.521

As you come out of the turn, your kart should be charged for a Super Mini-Turbo. Straighten out and release your drift to gain a nice burst of speed. As you approach the panel in the center of the track, allow your momentum to carry you to the left. In the following lap, a ramp emerges at this location; for now, speed past the closed panel and follow the left lane under the bridge.

x5

x5

x5

START/FINISH

A

B

C

D

1 00:01.647

After you Rocket Start off the starting line, veer gently to the right. There are some conveniently placed coins along the curve's inside edge, so make sure you're in position to grab them.

8 00:27.797

If you time it properly, the Mushroom's boost should carry you back to the asphalt. Drift between the two pipes near the edge of the sand, and try to align your kart with the track. As soon as you reach the pavement, release your drift for a burst of speed as you complete the first lap.

TACTICS FOR LAPS 2 & 3

As you come out of the first curve of lap 2, look for the ramp at the track's center. Drive across the glide panel to soar over the bridge. Be sure to hop just before you take off to gain a little extra speed during your glide.

If needed, make small adjustments to your racing line to grab any conveniently located coins.

Grand Prix

A

You'll face some stiff competition for item boxes early in the race. As you approach the first curve, pay attention to the racers in front of you. If they're in position to clear out the item boxes, it's generally best to focus on the upcoming turn. As the pack thins out, you'll have a much easier time claiming items.

B

As you come out of the first curve, check your opponents' karts for equipped items. You should gain some ground as you drift through the turn, but devious racers can keep you at bay with newly acquired items. As you head under the bridge, check the track for dropped items. If you have a Banana handy, try placing it just past one of the dash panels. If you don't see any immediate dangers, this straightaway is a great place to draft behind other racers.

C

The ramp toward the course's end offers a convenient shortcut—provided you have a Mushroom handy. As you exit the tunnel, veer to the right and approach the ramp head-on. Boost across the sand, then hop from the ramp's top to gain a little extra speed when you land.

D

If you have an appropriate item, you can use the shortcut described in the "Time Trial" section. Before you venture onto the sand, check the Touch Screen for any dangerously armed opponents. An unanticipated attack can strand you off-road, making it very difficult to get back into the race. If you're not comfortable with the risk, you can still gain a lot of ground by cutting across the edge of the sand.

TIP

Your opponents will often avoid the coins along the track's outside edge; if you haven't collected 10 coins by your third lap, make a wide drift through the last curve to scoop up any remaining coins on your way to the finish line.

Mirror Mode

When you race this course in Mirror mode, use all of the same tactics described here—just do so in the opposite direction. Every left turn becomes a right one (and vice versa) when the course is flipped.

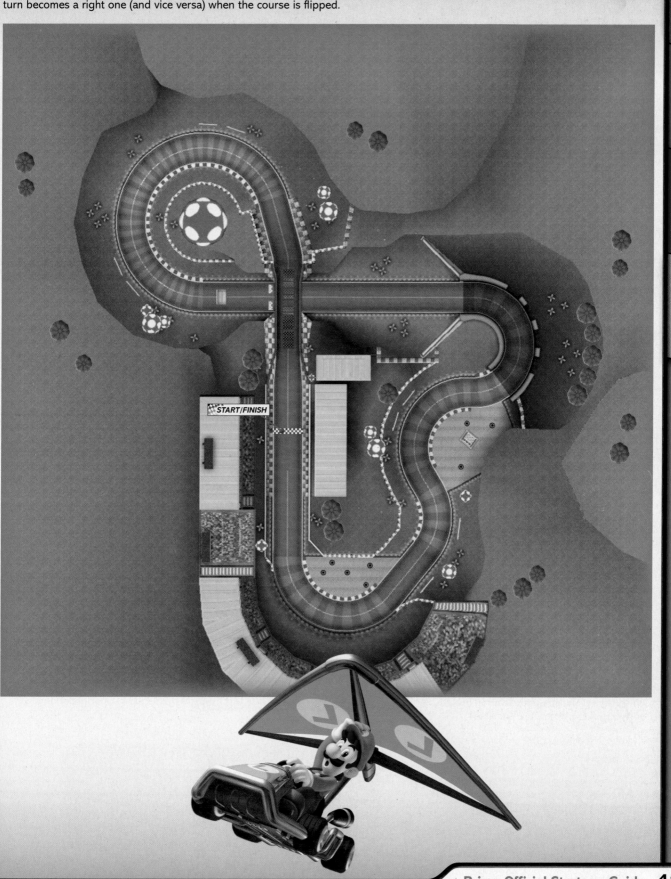

START/FINISH

Daisy Hills

Mushroom Cup

The setting may be idyllic, but there's no time for sightseeing! This seemingly simple course has several moving hazards, so make sure the road is clear before you commit to a drift. Keep your turns tight, and look for the hidden route off the beaten path.

ROAD HAZARDS

GRASS: Driving on grass slows you down! Unless you're able to boost through one of these patches, stick to the main path.

LAKE: Don't take a dip in this picturesque lake; even a quick plunge will cost you valuable time!

MOUNTAIN GOATS: These happy critters don't mean any harm, but they have a knack for wandering across your racing line. A high-speed collision results in a spinout and a lot of lost time.

PIPES: These off-road hazards can be hard to spot. If you venture onto the grass, take care to avoid these unforgiving obstacles.

HOT-AIR BALLOONS: These balloons may be a popular tourist attraction, but they can be big trouble for high-flying racers. Find a path through these floating obstacles.

WINDMILLS: Don't get caught up in their spinning blades—these windmills can bring your flight to an early end.

4

00:15.856

On the first lap, the mountain goats are fairly easy to avoid. Adjust your drift to slide past them, and try to charge a Super Mini-Turbo. As you cross the next bridge, try to collect the coins from the center of the path.

5

00:23.162

With a line of coins and numerous dash panels, the banked curve is an appealing option. However, for the fastest time, you'll want to drift along the track's inside edge. When you spot the two pipes near the edge of the grass, use a Mushroom to boost through the flower patch. Continue to follow the track's curve, but do so near the small fence on your left.

6

00:26.061

Your boost should carry you all the way to the hidden path across the grass. When you reach the dirt, release your drift to speed down the narrow runway. When you reach the glide panel, hop up to gain some extra speed as your glider unfolds.

CAUTION

Jump boosts are a great way to improve your time, but always weigh the risks against the rewards. If you hop too soon, you'll miss the glide panel altogether! You'll need your glider to cross the lake, so make sure you hit the glide panel before you hop.

Time Trial

THE KART OF CHAMPIONS

 Character: Daisy

Kart: Birthday Girl

Tires: Sponge

Glider: Super Glider

2

00:06.486

The path bends to the right at the small island. Use a wide drift to maintain your speed, but take care to avoid a costly fall. Try to charge another Mini-Turbo, but don't hesitate to release the drift if you're in danger of slipping into the water.

1

00:02.886

As you head into the first turn, drift to the left. If you stay near the grass, you can charge a Mini-Turbo by the time you round the corner. Release the drift and veer toward the bridge's right edge as you enjoy the small burst of speed.

3

00:11.122

When you spot the first log in the road, line up your kart to grab one of the coins above it. The log acts as a small ramp, launching your kart into the air. Perform a hop just as your wheels leave the ground to gain a small boost when your kart lands. Drift along the inside edge of the upcoming curve, and watch the road for roaming mountain goats.

?x5

?x4

Ⓑ

Ⓒ

Ⓐ

?x2

START/FINISH

Ⓓ

Ⓔ

?x6

Ⓕ

8

00:33.359

When you touch down on the main path, veer toward the coins to the right. Once you're lined up, drift through the coins and around the corner to charge up a Super Mini-Turbo. Release the drift as you round the corner for a nice boost as you complete the first lap.

7

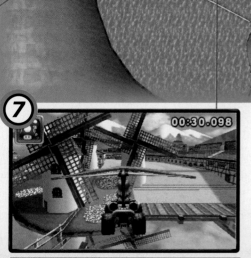

00:30.098

As you soar through the air, aim for the gap between the windmills. If the spinning blades are blocking your path, swoop down to slip under them, then pull back up to avoid landing on the grass.

Tactics for Laps 2 and 3

Use the same basic tactics to complete the remaining laps, but adjust your racing line to collect missed coins and avoid moving hazards. Perform big drifts to charge Mini-Turbos and Super Mini-Turbos, and use your remaining Mushrooms to cut over to the hidden path. Above all, make sure you stay out of that lake!

Grand Prix

If you're using a lightweight character and kart combination, be particularly careful as you cross the lake. Avoid jostling with other players, and try to claim one of the first four item boxes. If you receive a suitable item, equip it to protect yourself from heavier racers. If you're using a heavy character and kart combination, this is a great place to knock your smaller opponents into the water. When the path bends at the small island, draft behind any unarmed racers ahead of you; the boost you'll receive from a successful draft might just put you in an early lead.

The guardrails along the curved bridge make this an ideal spot to fire off a Green Shell. If you have one handy, use it to take out a leading opponent or toss it behind you to fend off encroaching racers. A stray attack has an excellent chance of ricocheting into a random target, so fire away!

If you've managed to collect a Mushroom during the race, cut across the grass to use the hidden path. Most of your opponents stick to the main track, so you have a great shot at collecting one of the item boxes along the alternate route. However, if you don't have a way to boost across the grass, consider drifting up to the banked strip to the right. The extra coins can be a great help in the remaining laps, and the numerous dash panels prevent you from losing too much ground.

During a Grand Prix cup, the hot-air balloons move quite a bit. You shouldn't have too much trouble finding an opening along the main track, but use caution when you take the hidden path. You may not have much time to adjust, so be ready to swerve as you drive across the glide panel.

With the right item equipped, you can cause a lot of trouble for airborne opponents. Triple Red Shells or Triple Green Shells can turn a basic jostle into a race-changing attack, and a well-timed Lightning strike can devastate multiple racers. It can be extremely satisfying to send tenacious opponents into the lake—just remember that the same tactics can be used against you!

If you follow the main path back across the lake, dodge the windmill blades and touch down on the track. Use the fountain at the lap's final turn to perform a jump boost, then drift around the corner and Super Mini-Turbo along the straightaway. If you managed to take the hidden path, use the same tactics described in the "Time Trial" section.

Mirror Mode

Drift, glide, and battle your way across this flipped course. Use all of the previously described tactics, but take each turn in the opposite direction!

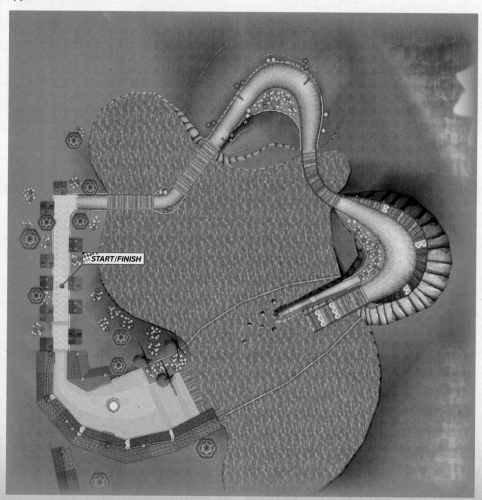

START/FINISH

Cheep Cheep Lagoon

Mushroom Cup

Prove that you're the best by land, sea, or air! Cheep Cheep Lagoon has something for everyone, but this course isn't all fun and games. From its giant Clampys to its scuttling Sidesteppers, Cheep Cheep Lagoon has its share of hazards. Take care when you hit the water; a proper entry is the key to victory!

ROAD HAZARDS

GRASS: If you veer off the track, you may spend a little more time on dry land than you intended. Unless you have a Mushroom handy, keep off the grass!

ROCKS: Keep an eye out for these jagged obstacles. Your kart performs differently in the water—plan ahead to avoid costly crashes.

CHEEP CHEEPS: These familiar fish aren't looking for trouble. As long as you stay out of a Cheep Cheep's path, it's happy to swim right past you.

CHASM: Your kart wasn't designed for deep-sea exploration! Keep out of this murky abyss if you hope to claim victory.

CLAMPY: These snapping Clampys bait their prey with coins and item boxes. Before you snag one of these tempting prizes, make sure you can escape the Clampy's snapping jaws.

SIDESTEPPERS: These unpredictable crabs have a knack for getting in your way. Give them a wide berth to avoid unfortunate spinouts!

STALACTITES: If you choose to take the high road, watch out for these low-hanging hazards!

② As you approach the dash panel, aim for the coin to the right. Approach the coin from a slight angle, but steer clear of the support beams below the large sign. Remember to hop from the edge of the dash panel; this provides a small burst of speed when you hit the water. While in the air, push up on the Circle Pad to tilt your kart downward. When you reach the maximum angle, release the Circle Pad.

① Drift around the first turn, and try to charge a Mini-Turbo. If you pick a proper angle, you should have one ready by the time you reach the wooden ramp. Release the drift for a burst of speed, then grab a coin as you race across the planks.

⑧ Drift into the final turn, then use a Mushroom to cut across the strip of grass. As the boost ends, release your drift to speed through the end of the lap.

NOTE

The Clampys along the ocean floor produce coins and item boxes at regular intervals.

⑦ Dodge the Sidesteppers along the floor, then continue across the dash panels to return to dry land. Remember to hop just as you surface—the extra boost of speed is a big help in the final stretch!

Time Trial

THE KART OF CHAMPIONS

 Character: Peach

Kart: Tiny Tug

Tires: Roller

Glider: Peach Parasol

When you hit the water at this angle, your kart takes much longer to reach the ocean floor. This helps maintain your speed and allows you to float over a large rock that would otherwise block your path.

4 00:12.838

If you've managed to clear the rock, you should touch down on a slight incline. Veer toward the narrow ledge to the right, and hop from the top of the bump to gain a small boost. There's a large chasm to the right, so use caution as you drive along the ledge.

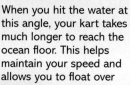

3 00:10.902

x5

(B)

(C)

(A)

START/FINISH

x1

(D)

(E)

x2

x1

x3

x1

5 00:14.770

The ledge isn't that long, but the shortcut can shave several seconds off your completion time. As you drop down from the ledge's end, avoid the nearby Clampy. Follow a smooth racing line down the center of the path, but look for a chance to grab a coin from a freshly opened Clampy.

6 00:23.236

When you exit the water, head straight down the wide path as it curves through the center of the cavern. Grab one of the coins ahead of you, then hop from the ramp at the path's end. Once again, tilt your kart toward the water, then release the Circle Pad before you splash down.

INTRODUCTION · NEW CUPS · CLASSIC CUPS · BATTLE MAPS

Tactics for Laps 2 and 3

Use the same basic tactics for the remaining laps. Focus on clean transitions from dry land to water, and adjust your racing line to snag any conveniently located coins.

Grand Prix

Try to jostle for one of the item boxes near the start of the race. It can be tough to grab one before the competition thins out, but an early item can be a big help.

As you enter the water, aggressive opponents might knock you out of the ideal position. Depending on your priorities, you can collect the coins along the main path or use the inclines to jump up to the ledge. The ledge offers temporary protection from most enemy attacks, but hoarding coins can pay off in the remaining laps. If you choose to stay on the main path, hop from the top of each incline to help keep your speed up—just make sure you check for overhead Cheep Cheeps!

Remember to check the Clampys for additional item boxes. If you're confident you can grab one, do so! Most opponents should be unarmed at this point, and a fresh item can give you a real edge.

As you enter the cavern, check the Touch Screen for nearby racers. If you see an opponent heading for the narrow path on the left, try to draft behind them. As your speed picks up, you should be able to knock them into the water. This is also a great spot to drop a Banana or fire off a Green Shell. Of course, other racers can also use these tactics. Stay alert!

If you stick to the main path, use the tactics described in the "Time Trial" section. If you follow the narrow path on the left, hop from the edge of the glide panel, then steer your kart through the stalactites as you glide above the water.

Mirror Mode

The turns have changed but the tactics remain! Veer, turn, and drift in the opposite directions to battle your way to victory.

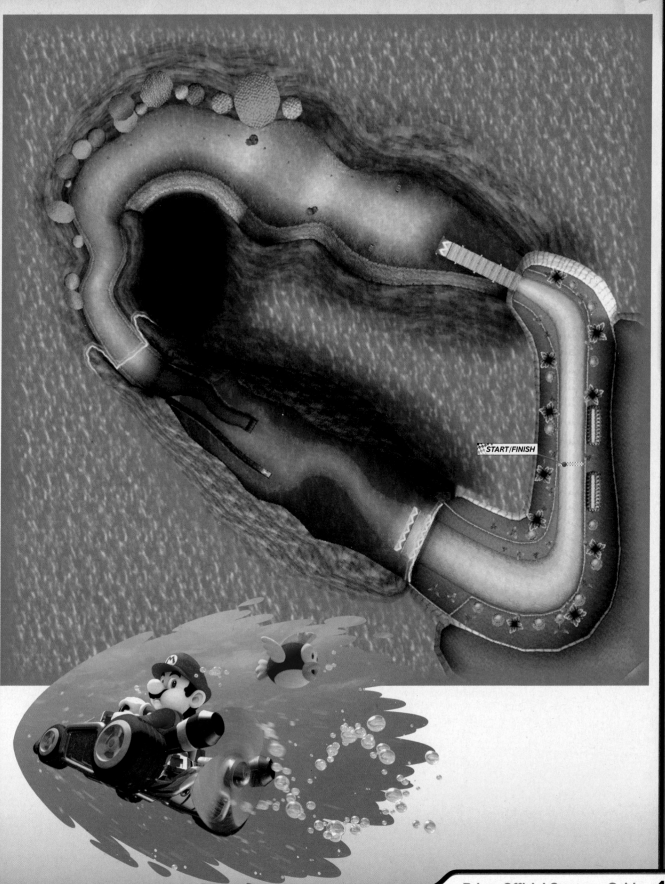

START/FINISH

Shy Guy Bazaar

Mushroom Cup

Expect danger around every corner as you head through this desert village. Weave a path through the outdoor market, then make a daring dash across the rooftops. It's a beautiful night, but danger lurks around each corner of Shy Guy Bazaar!

ROAD HAZARDS

 DEEP SAND: Much of the course is dusted with sand, but the deep sand lining much of track is more than your kart can handle! Unless you have a Mushroom handy, stay on the indicated path.

 STEEP DROPS: This course has several steep drops! When you cross a bridge or dash over the rooftops, make sure your kart is heading for solid ground.

 STALLS: These merchant stalls are sturdier than they look! Swerve around them or head over them to stay in the race.

 URNS: This course is filled with large urns—avoid them all. Pay special attention to the urns placed directly on the track; these hazards change positions when they think no one is watching!

 FLYING SHY GUYS: Avoid crossing paths with these Shy Guys! A midair collision can ruin a lovely glide.

3

As you get into position, drift back to the left and grab the coin as you slide around the closest red stall. Use a second drift to swing by the yellow stall on your right. With proper timing, you should be able to Mini-Turbo as you change directions. Follow the wall on your right, and look for the upcoming covered walkway.

2

As you cross the bridge, begin a new drift and follow the path at it curves to the right. You'll notice a small dash panel along the far wall, but you'll save a lot of time if you stay on the ground. Hold the drift until you charge a Super Mini-Turbo, then head toward for the coin located near the dash panel.

1

Just off the starting line, the course bends to the right, then curves back to the left. Drift into the bend, then release the drift and start a new one in the opposite direction. Try to charge a Mini-Turbo through with each drift to gain speed as you enter the village.

Time Trial

THE KART OF CHAMPIONS

- Character: Shy Guy
- Kart: Pipe Frame
- Tires: Monster
- Glider: Paraglider

4

Head straight for the coins inside the walkway, then drift through them as the path curves to the right. Hold the drift as you pass over the dash panel. When you reach the next turn, release the drift for a Super Mini-Turbo.

5

Drift through the next turn, then boost into the straightaway. There are three urns at the center of the path, so take care to dodge them. Begin a slight drift to the right, and hold it as you slip past the urns. Maintain the drift through the upcoming turn, then Super Mini-Turbo through into the next straightaway.

6

Stay near the path's left edge, and grab the two coins straight ahead of you. Continue up the ramp, over the dash panel, and across the rooftops. Each time you reach the top of a ramp, remember to hop for an extra boost.

7

Drive across the glide panel on the last rooftop, then hop up to barrel roll as your glider unfolds. Try to grab at least one of the coins ahead of you, but keep an eye out for flying Shy Guys.

8

When you land, drift along the path as it curves to the right. Watch for the two large urns at the next corner, then use a Mushroom to boost between them. As you return to the main path, release your drift to Super Mini-Turbo toward the end of the lap.

x5

x5

x5

START/FINISH

A
B
C
D
E

Tactics for Laps 2 and 3

Use the same basic tactics to complete the remaining laps. The urns don't move during the Time Trial, but the flying Shy Guys certainly do! Adjust your racing line to avoid moving hazards, and try to collect any conveniently located coins.

Grand Prix

C

If you're using a lighter racer, beware of jostling on the bridge. It's great if you manage to grab an item box, but it won't do you much good if you're knocked clear off the path. Heavier racers have a clear advantage at this location. The bridge is also a great spot to drop Bananas during the remaining laps.

Keep a watchful eye on the smaller urns along the path. During a Grand Prix race, you'll find them scooting into your path. If you see a pair of eyes peeking out from under the lid, keep your distance! Heavier racers can gain an advantage by jostling nearby opponents into these obstacles.

TIP

The sharp curves throughout this area are ideal for Banana drops or Green Shell ricochets! If you get the chance, use one of these items as you drift through a turn.

The stalls offer plenty of great locations to drop a Banana or ricochet a Green Shell. Your opponents are sure to have similar plans, so use the Touch Screen to locate nearby threats as you head into the bazaar. If the main path is too cluttered for comfort, slip into the walkway along the right wall, or use the dash panel near the village entrance to take the high path through the market.

The rooftops provide several tactical options. Place a Banana at the top of a ramp, or jump across the gap and drop one when you land. The narrow path doesn't offer much room to dodge; even if a player avoids your trap, it may force them into a nearby obstacle. Lightning strikes are a real worry for airborne racers. If you manage to collect one of these rare items, use it while an opponent is approaching a ramp or gliding back down from the rooftops.

You shouldn't have much trouble collecting coins, but hanging on to them can be challenging! If you need to replace lost coins, look for them as you approach the finish line. If you spot one, chances are you'll find a few more on the nearby steps.

Mirror Mode

Don't get lost as you weave through the stalls! Use the same tactics in Mirror mode—just flip the direction of each drift and turn.

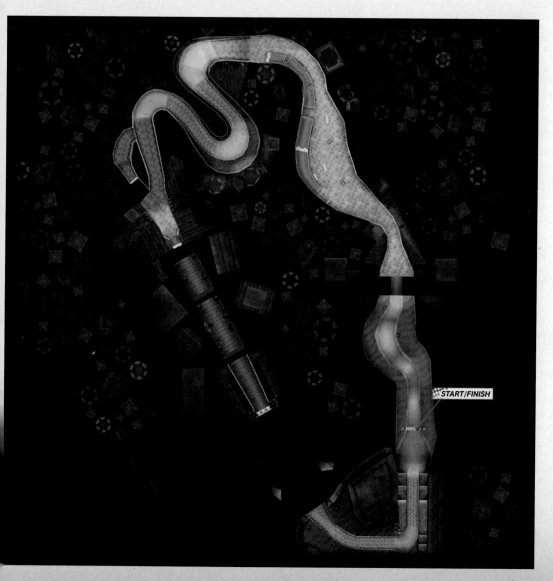

START/FINISH

Wuhu Loop

Flower Cup

Drift, jump, and boost your way through Wuhu Loop! The track provides the fastest route, but alternate paths put your glider to good use. Unlike most events, this race takes place over one long lap. The course is divided into three sections, so use the Touch Screen to monitor your progress. If you're not in the lead by the time you reach section 3, it's time to pick up the pace!

ROAD HAZARDS

GRASS: By now you know that driving on the grass slows you down. On this course, however, the grass contains several other dangers. Obstacles like trees and signs will stop you in your tracks. If you venture too far off-road, you might just find yourself tumbling off the map! As always, you can use Mushrooms to boost across the grass—just make sure you have a clear path back to the road.

OCEAN: This island course takes you through some perilous turns. An unfortunate fall can cost you the race; mind your drifts and glides!

VEHICLES: Keep your distance from slow-moving cars and trucks; your kart is no match for these full-sized vehicles!

TRAFFIC BARRIERS: Steer clear of the traffic barriers placed throughout the course. Although these obstacles are intended to prevent accidents, you may find they have the opposite effect!

CRATES: A high-speed collision will smash these crates, but it will also bring your kart to a stop. Avoid them!

⑨ As you enter section 3, use all of the same tactics to maintain your speed. Drift through each curve, and hop from the ramps along the road to gain useful jump boosts. When the course leads you back to the island's edge, be mindful of sheer drops—particularly if you risk drifting onto a precariously placed ramp!

④ Dodge past any vehicles near the tunnel entrance, then begin a gentle drift as the road curves to the left. It's best to stay near the curve's outside edge, but avoid the pillars that appear on your right. It's difficult to maintain a drift in this area, but try to pull off at least one Mini-Turbo. Grab a couple of the coins near the exit, then prepare to drift through the next turn.

⑩ When you reach the crates in the road, you're on the last stretch to the finish line. If you've managed to hang on to at least one of your Mushrooms, look for the ramp near the last crate. If you wish, veer to the left, then boost across the grass and over the ramp; remember to hop into the jump for a small boost! If you'd rather stick to the road, drift through the next two turns, then Super Mini-Turbo over one of the final ramps. Hop into the jump, then use any remaining Mushrooms to boost to the finish line.

① The key to a fast time is to drift through virtually every curve. Don't be fooled; this simple strategy is surprisingly dangerous! Much of the course runs along the island's outside edge, and uncontrolled drifts can send you right off the track. Whenever possible, start your drift early to ensure a smooth turn. You have a chance to practice this on the track's first bend. As you approach it, initiate a gentle drift, then steer your kart onto the bridge.

② Drive down the center of the bridge and through the coin at the ramp's top. Hop just before the jump to gain a small boost when you land, then drift gently to the right. Hold the drift through the next curve, release it for a Mini-Turbo, then drift back to the left to charge up another boost.

Time Trial

THE KART OF CHAMPIONS

 Character: Peach

 Kart: Pipe Frame

 Tires: Slick

 Glider: Peach Parasol

CAUTION

When using this shortcut in Time Trial mode, avoid hopping between pillars! The boost from the dash panel gives you just enough speed to skip across each gap.

8 00:59.183

There's a risky shortcut toward the end of section 2. It can shave some time off of your lap, but it's not for the faint of heart! The track curves around three pillars that you can use to cut across the gap. To do so, drift toward the pillars and approach them head-on. Drive off the track and onto the dash panel, then let the boost carry you across the remaining pillars. If you're not comfortable doing this, stick to the road. Drift through the coins and around the curve, then use a Super Mini-Turbo to help make up for lost time.

7  00:53.073

Drift along the path as it curves to the left, then Mini-Turbo toward the second ramp. Aim for the coin on the left, then hop from the ramp's top to gain a jump boost. As you return to the road, keep an eye out for slower vehicles.

 x4

x2

D x4 C

x1

B

SECTION 3

E x4 x4

SECTION 2

x2

x2

F

START/FINISH x4

A

6  00:47.803

When you see the first awning, veer to the left, then drift along the road as it curves to the right. Try to hold the drift long enough to charge a Mini-Turbo, but make sure you stay near the road's left edge. As you come out of the turn, veer onto the small path beneath the awnings. Drive over the first ramp, then hop into the jump to gain a small boost.

3  00:17.871

As the road straightens out, release your drift to Mini-Turbo, then look for the ramp near the inside edge of the next turn. Veer to the right, then use a Mushroom to boost across the grass. As you near the ramp, adjust your angle for a proper approach. Drive over the ramp and hop into the jump for a small boost as you return to the road. When you land, drift through the left turn to charge a Super Mini-Turbo on your way to the end of section 1

5  00:38.042

Begin a drift as the road curves to the right. You should be able to charge a Mini-Turbo before the road cuts back to the left, but don't get greedy! If you hold the drift too long, you may find yourself tumbling into the ocean. As you reach the next curve, release the drift and start a fresh one in the opposite direction. As the track takes you back inland, perform a series of small drifts to boost through each curve. Grab any coins you see, and look for the awnings coming up on your left.

Alternate Tactics

If precision drifting isn't for you, consider using the alternate routes detailed in the Grand Prix section. These routes aren't quite as fast, but they're certainly fun! With a little planning, you can glide your way to an impressive completion time.

Grand Prix

When the race begins, try to draft behind any of the racers ahead of you. Since none of your opponents have an item yet, this is a great place to practice this technique. If you pull it off, you can push your way to an early lead and claim one of the item boxes near the bridge. Pay special attention to any opponents driving close to the ledge. Jostle them as you pass by to knock them off the track! There are plenty of steep drops along the course, so look for similar opportunities as the race progresses.

The tunnel is a great spot to drop a Banana or ricochet a Green Shell. Bananas are particularly effective when there are vehicles in the area; your opponents are much more likely to fall into your trap when they're forced to avoid slow-moving traffic.

The road offers the fastest route through the area, but your opponents can make it difficult to drift through dangerous turns. If you're getting bullied on the ground, consider taking to the skies! Look for the hidden tunnel in section 2. As you drive along the island's edge, stay to the right. When the course leads back inland, watch for the tunnel, then drop down and head inside. Drive over the glide panel at the path's end, hop up to perform a barrel roll, then glide back to the road.

The second glide panel is located about halfway through section 3. Look for the dirt path leading off to the right, then follow it toward the lighthouse. After you cross the first dash panel, the path curves to the left. Drift through the next dash panel, then Super Mini-Turbo to the glide panel at the path's end. Hop into the jump to gain a small boost as you begin your glide.

As you glide, look for the large fan floating above the ocean. Cross over the current to extend your glide, and veer back toward the road. When you land, drift, draft, and boost your way to the finish line!

Mirror Mode

Drifts and Mini-Turbos are just as effective, but you need to make one small adjustment: All of the turns are reversed in Mirror mode!

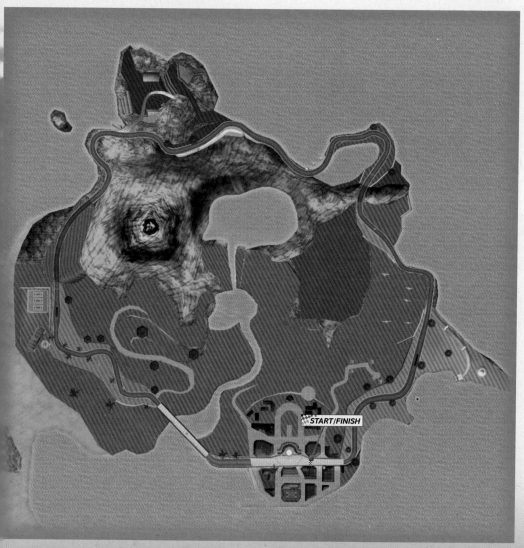

START/FINISH

INTRODUCTION

NEW CUPS

CLASSIC CUPS

BATTLE MAPS

Mario Circuit
Flower Cup

Drift, bounce, jump, and glide your way through Mario Circuit! Race through the castle grounds, then head inside for a spin up a spiraling ramp. Dodge through the Goombas and pipes on your way through the garden, and keep your kart out of the castle moat!

ROAD HAZARDS

GRASS: Keep off the grass to keep up your speed! Aside from the standard slowing effect, the grass along this course contains several trees. Boost through the grass or steer around it!

CASTLE MOAT: If you stay on track, you'll hardly notice the castle moat, but a botched drift or unfortunate jostle can end in a sudden fall.

GOOMBAS: These grumpy Goombas are looking for trouble. Keep your distance.

PIPES: No good can come from crashing into a pipe. Watch the road and steer to safety.

1

As you enter the first curve, drift through the two coins along its inside edge. Make sure you stay off the grass! If you slip down the decline, you'll wind up in the castle moat. Super Mini-Turbo out of the turn, then begin a new drift as the track curves to the right. After you charge a second Super Mini-Turbo, use it to boost into the long, tree-lined strip of track.

3

When you land, use a Mushroom to boost straight through the grass. You can veer onto the ramp, but it's generally faster to maintain your heading. After you reach the path, follow it into the castle and up the looping ramp.

2

As the track curves to the left, perform a drift to charge another Super Mini-Turbo. As you come out of the turn, release the drift to boost toward the ramp ahead of you. Hop from the ramp's top to gain a jump boost, then hop again as you bounce off of the giant mushroom.

Time Trial

THE KART OF CHAMPIONS

Character: Mario

Kart: B Dasher

Tires: Slick

Glider: Super Glider

⑦ 00:40.028

Follow the path into the pipe tunnel and drift through the turn. Follow the coins along the center of the path, then release the drift to boost into the straightaway. Hop from the large bump in the road to gain a jump boost as you complete the lap.

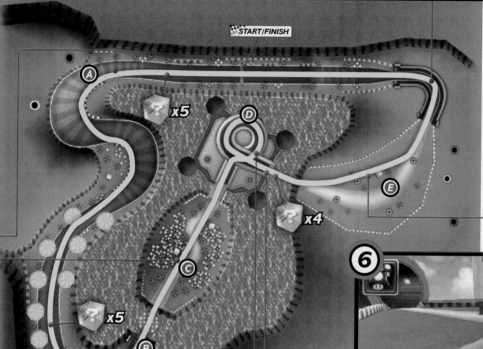

START/FINISH

Ⓐ

x5

Ⓓ

Ⓔ

x4

Ⓒ

x5

Ⓑ

⑥ 00:35.692

Glide above the grass along the path's left edge. Pass over the pipe, and touch down on the ramp. If you land cleanly, your glider will carry you to the path.

④ 00:27.466

Drift through the coins in the center of the path and charge up a Super Mini-Turbo. As you exit the curve, release the drift to boost into the straightaway.

⑤ 00:31.887

Drive straight to the path's end, and hop from the edge of the glide panel. Veer slightly to the left as you glide across the moat and into the garden.

INTRDOUCION

NEW CUPS

CLASSIC CUPS

BATTLE MAPS

Tactics for Laps 2 and 3

Use the same basic tactics to complete the remaining laps, but adjust your racing line to collect any conveniently located coins. When you glide down from the castle, look for the air current blowing out of the garden pipe. Aim for the ramp just like you did on the first lap, but note that the gust from the pipe should carry you all the way to the path.

Grand Prix

Be careful as you head into the first turn! After passing through the nearby item boxes, several of your opponents are now armed. If a nearby racer has equipped an item, you could find yourself on the losing end of a jostle. Try to charge a Super Mini-Turbo, but don't get caught by a surprise attack.

Unless you just picked up a Mushroom at the race's start, you should adjust your angle as you jump to the giant mushroom. Stay slightly to the right to ensure you land on the path. Try to grab a couple of coins on your way into the castle, but stay off of the grass.

The looping ramp inside the castle is a great place to use an item. Drop a Banana as you drift through the center of the path, or toss a Green Shell behind you to keep encroaching racers at bay.

When you glide down from the castle, try to use the tactics described in the "Time Trial" section. If an aggressive opponent forces you to make an emergency landing, take care when you drive through the garden. Stay to the left to avoid the pipe near the path's edge, and keep an eye on those lumbering Goombas.

Mirror Mode

The same tactics apply, but you'll need to relearn them for Mirror mode—all of the turns are flipped!

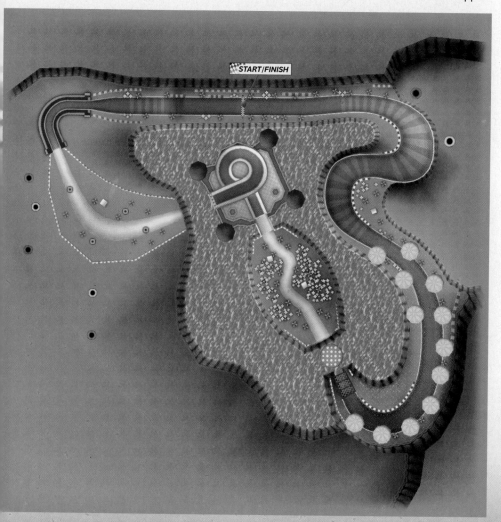

START/FINISH

Music Park

Flower Cup

Race through the blaring horns, crashing cymbals, and pulsing speakers of this exhilarating course. Play along with the music as you drift across giant keyboards, but be sure to avoid slipping off the track. Piranha Plants dance and musical notes bounce to the beat. In Music Park, everyone gets in on the act!

ROAD HAZARDS

GRASS: Unless you have a Mushroom in hand, stay away from these patches of grass.

DROPS: Don't get carried away by the music; sliding off the track will cost you valuable time!

PIRANHA PLANTS: These Piranha Plants aren't willing to share the spotlight. Keep away from their snapping jaws.

BOUNCING NOTES: These musical notes bounce along to the music—make sure you're out of the way when they come crashing down!

⑧ The musical notes bounce from side to side, but each one stays inside its marked area. Glide along the track's edge until your kart touches down. Each time the notes hit the track, the impact bounces you into the air. When this happens, perform a jump boost to gain a little extra speed on your way through the area. Drift through the next two turns, then Super Mini-Turbo your way to the end of the lap.

⑦

⑥

⑥ Super Mini-Turbo toward the dash panel, and aim your kart toward the coins along the next curve's inside edge. Hop into the jump, then hop again as you bounce from the tambourine. When you land, drift through the coins and follow the track as it curves to the right.

As you come out of the turn, look for the two ramps just ahead of you. The ramps alternate positions; as one ramp tilts upward, the other one lowers. Each ramp contains a glide panel that activates only when it's in the higher position, so adjust your racing line as needed. Super Mini-Turbo along the track's center, then veer onto the active glide panel to deploy your glider. Remember to hop just before you take off!

⑤

⑤ Keep your drift fairly tight, but avoid the raised keys along the inside edge. You can fall from either side of the keyboard, so try to stay near the track's center. As you exit the turn, Super Mini-Turbo toward the gray keyboard, then repeat the process as you drift back to the left.

Time Trial

THE KART OF CHAMPIONS

 Character: Rosalina

 Kart: Soda Jet

 Tires: Roller

 Glider: Paraglider

INTRODUCTION
NEW CUPS
CLASSIC CUPS
BATTLE MAPS

①  00:02.464

Drift through the first bend, but don't worry too much about charging a Mini-Turbo. It's much more important to focus on the loop ahead of you. Hop up and start a new drift as the track curves to the left.

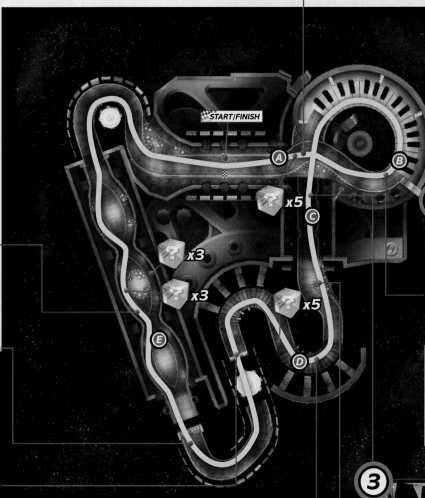

START/FINISH

Ⓐ Ⓑ Ⓒ Ⓓ Ⓔ

x5 x3 x3 x5

② 00:05.751

Stay near the loop's inside edge, but take care to avoid falling off the track. Hold the drift on your way across the keyboard, then Super Mini-Turbo into the straightaway. The spotlights ahead of you indicate the current locations of two Piranha Plants, so adjust your angle to avoid them.

③ 00:11.919

Use the line down the track's center to gauge the range of the Piranha Plants. As long as you stay in the opposite lane, you can safely cut through the edge of each spotlight. As you approach the second Piranha Plant, veer toward the grass patch coming up on your left.

④  00:14.423

Line your kart up with the ramp, and use a Mushroom to boost across the grass. Hop from the ramp's top, then drift onto the brown keyboard as it curves to the right.

Grand Prix

Stick to the left as you approach the first group of item boxes. You can expect some heavy jostling, so it's best to stay away from the grass patch. As you approach the keyboard, veer to the right to avoid being knocked off the track.

As you drift along the first keyboard, keep your distance from the inside edge. If your opponents are particularly aggressive, consider jump boosting along the raised keys or using the banked strip. A Super Mini-Turbo is your best chance at an early lead, but it's more important to avoid a costly fall!

The Piranha Plants love snapping at reckless racers. Each time you pass through this area, look for coins dropped by overeager opponents.

Although it can be satisfying to knock an opponent off the track, it's generally best to avoid jostling along the keyboards. If the other racers aren't causing trouble, focus on performing clean drifts—you'll have plenty of chances to battle your foes in less dangerous areas.

As you glide past the bouncing notes, look for the item boxes flanking the grass patch. If your opponents are clearing out one of the lanes, move to the track's other side. You have a great view of the area from up here—put it to good use!

Mirror Mode

If you remember to flip each of your turns, you won't miss a beat on this Mirror mode track!

Rock Rock Mountain

Flower Cup

Climb, glide, and drift your way around this majestic mountaintop. The course is fairly simple, but the varied terrain can challenge even the most experienced racer. From startled Swoopers to bounding boulders, this track has its share of hazards. Stay alert, and don't let your opponents push you around; it's a long way down from the top of this mountain!

ROAD HAZARDS

 GRASS: Driving on the grass will slow you down, but hitting a tree will stop you cold! Unless you're boosting through a clearing, avoid grassy areas.

 STEEP DROPS: A quick trip down the mountainside will cost you valuable time. Be careful!

 SWOOPERS: Swooper colonies don't take kindly to rowdy racers. Dodge around these cavern-dwelling creatures.

 ROCK COLUMNS: Avoid costly collisions! Steer around these rock columns.

 PIPES: You'll find plenty of pipes along this course. Be sure to avoid them as you glide down to the forest.

 TRAFFIC CONES: Your kart can knock these minor obstacles out of your path, but it's best to avoid them.

 BOULDERS: Watch out for falling rocks! These massive boulders bounce as they roll down the mountain. When you spot one, make sure you move out of its path.

③

②

As you enter the cavern, watch out for incoming Swoopers. Try to drift along the wall to the right, but swing wide if you don't have enough space. When you come out of the turn, release the drift and Super Mini-Turbo toward the wall to your left. Make sure to avoid the first rock column, then drift through the coins as the path snakes through the cavern.

①

Rocket Start off the line, then veer to the left. Drift back to the right and grab the coins near the path's edge. Try to hold the drift long enough to charge a Super Mini-Turbo, but make sure you don't fall off the mountain! As the path curves to the left, release your drift and start a new one. Try to perform at least one more Super Mini-Turbo before you reach the cavern entrance.

⑨

As you drive over the dash panel, scan the area for incoming boulders. If the path is clear, boost straight to the next dash panel, then return to the path's center. Keep an eye out for boulders, and use the available dash panels to speed up the mountainside. When you reach the glide panel, hop into the jump and glide through the end of the lap.

Time Trial

THE KART OF CHAMPIONS

 Character: Wiggler

Kart: Standard

Tires: Mushroom

Glider: Flower Glider

4 00:17.879

Exit the cavern and drive straight down the metal ramp. Aim for the center of the glide panel, then hop into the jump to barrel roll as your glider deploys.

5 00:23.774

Glide through the coins in your path, but watch out for the pipe protruding from the rocks on your right. As you approach the second group of coins, veer slightly to the left to avoid the pipe on your way down to the forest. When you land, follow the path to another glide panel. This glide is much shorter than the first one; swoop under the toppled tree ahead of you and return to the path.

6 00:36.244

Land in the path's center, then drift into a hard right turn. Look for the small ramp in the grass ahead of you, then use a Mushroom to boost through the clearing.

x4

x4

A

B

START/FINISH

D

C

x1

x5

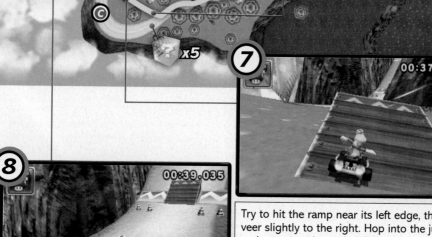
7 00:37.711

8 00:39.035

Try to hit the ramp near its left edge, then veer slightly to the right. Hop into the jump and return to the path. When you land, veer toward the dash panel coming up on your left. Try to slip through the gap between the traffic cones and the ramp, but straighten out to avoid boosting into the wall.

INTRODUCTION · NEW CUPS · CLASSIC CUPS · BATTLE MAPS

Tactics for Laps 2 and 3

Use the same basic tactics to complete the remaining laps. Adjust your racing line to dodge new Swoopers and boulders, and try to grab any conveniently placed coins.

Grand Prix

The steep drop near the race's start is obviously much more dangerous with opponents in the mix. There's bound to be plenty of jostling at the race's start, so take steps to protect yourself; stay near the center of the track to ensure you survive early collisions.

When you can't boost through the grass, make sure you perform a jump boost from the ramp in the path. It's not nearly as effective as the shortcut, but it's your best option when you don't have a Mushroom.

The climb back up the mountain is another great spot to drop Bananas. If you have one, try to place it just after one of the dash panels along the path's center. Most racers will cross over both of these as they boost up the path, so you have an excellent chance of catching someone in your trap.

The cavern is a great place to use a Green Shell—particularly if you have one on the first lap. If you have a Banana, drop it near the cavern exit; the narrow passage makes it much harder to dodge. Your opponents are likely to use these tactics against you, so use the Touch Screen to check for items hidden around blind corners.

Mirror Mode

You'll drift and glide just as before, and the bouncing boulders are just as dangerous. The same basic tactics apply, but you'll need to adjust them to match this track's flipped turns.

START/FINISH

Piranha Plant Slide

Star Cup

Take a wild ride through this high-speed course! Get a boost from the flowing water, but don't let the currents knock you off course. Watch out for the hungry Piranha Plants and waddling Goombas along the track. Several item boxes are on the move; you'll have to go with the flow to catch them!

ROAD HAZARDS

GRASS: Most of the race takes place in the water, but you'll find some grass near the end of each lap. Unless you have a Mushroom handy, stick to the main path!

STEEP DROPS: These big drops can ruin a big lead. Stay on track as you race through the sewers.

PIRANHA PLANTS: You don't have much room to dodge these Piranha Plants. Be careful!

GOOMBAS: Steer around these slow-moving Goombas. A collision will cost you valuable time.

CURRENTS: These currents won't do much harm, but they can push you off your racing line. If you pass through one, use some quick steering to compensate.

DRAIN PIPES: The pipes aren't much of a problem, but the water flowing from them is another matter. Weave through the downpour to maintain your glide.

NOTE

New item boxes regularly appear in the flowing water. Look for them as you race through the sewer.

④ 00:15.992

Look for the dash panels near the upcoming drop, then pull onto the walkway to your left. Drive straight across the dash panel; you're aiming for the coins ahead of you. After you land, drive through the coins and drop to the ground.

⑤ 00:19.589

As you approach the next turn, veer to the right and drift back to the left. Be careful! You'll lose a lot of time if you slip off the path. Drift gently at first, then adjust your angle as you round the corner. Try to charge a Super Mini-Turbo before you come out of the turn; the extra boost will help keep you on the track. Drift through the next turn, then follow the path into the underwater corridor.

⑥ 00:29.127

Through the first half of the corridor, try to drift down the path's center. As you head through the curve, veer toward the right wall. Maintain your drift as you drive across the dash panel, but stay close to the wall. Ride the boost past the Piranha Plant, then release the drift to Super Mini-Turbo toward the exit. When you reach the glide panel, hop into a barrel roll and glide down the center of the path.

⑧ 00:37.451

Try to avoid the water pouring out of the drain pipes. You lose altitude each time you pass through a downpour, so it's important to limit your contact. As you approach the ledge, aim for the small bush in the grass ahead of you.

⑦ 00:31.885

Time Trial

THE KART OF CHAMPIONS

 Character: Lakitu

 Kart: Cloud 9

 Tires: Sponge

Glider: Paraglider

③ 00:12.627

Drift through the small bends, and focus on staying in the water. As you approach the next turn, veer to the right, then make a hard drift to the left. Resist the urge to cut across the walkway! The Goombas are easy enough to dodge, but you'll move much faster if you stay in the water. As you come out of the turn, Super Mini-Turbo into the straightaway.

② 00:07.551

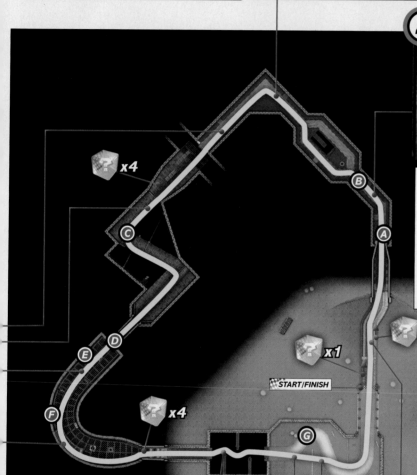

As you surface, hop from the ramp's edge, then make a hard drift to the left. Try to stay near the path's center to take advantage of the flowing water. As you turn the corner, look for the Piranha Plant ahead of you. Maintain your drift as long as possible, then Super Mini-Turbo toward the narrow walkway on your left. The Piranha Plant has quite a range, so keep your distance until you pass it.

TIP

If you see the Piranha Plant snap as you approach, consider staying in the water; you should be able to speed past while it readies its next attack.

① 00:01.822

As you head over the ramp near the start of the lap, hop into the jump to gain a small boost. When you land, drive through the water at the track's center. When the track dips down, maintain your heading and hop from the top of the decline. As the course bends to the right, you should land in the water along the left edge. After you plunge into the deep water, stay to the left.

⑨ 00:39.987

⑩ 00:40.618

When you land, maintain your heading. Use a Mushroom to boost straight across the grass. After you smash through the bush, continue through the small gap in the fence. This shortcut saves time, and it's the easiest way to avoid the wandering Goomba. You return to the track just as it curves to the left. Drift through the turn, then Mini-Turbo toward the end of the lap.

Grand Prix

Remember to watch the water for roaming item boxes. If you collect a few of these on each lap, you'll have a big advantage over most of your opponents!

The Piranha Plants are much more aggressive in the Grand Prix mode. As you approach the first Piranha Plant, note the direction it's facing. Make sure you take the other path!

If you have a Banana, consider dropping it as you drift through this sharp turn. You might end up sending an unfortunate racer right off the track! Remember that your opponents are bound to use the same tactic.

The path into the underwater corridor is another great spot to lay a trap. Be prepared to dodge any Bananas left by your opponents, and look for the chance to drop one yourself.

If your opponents force you to the edge of the underwater corridor, remember to hop each time you drive over a pipe. The jump boosts you gain should prevent you from losing too much ground. Note that the various currents switch on and off as the race progresses. If the current near the right wall is active, use it to reach the coins on the high ledge.

Two of the Goombas near the end of each lap are actually decoys, so you can smash through them when needed. Watch out for the real Goomba—this roaming baddie can knock you right out of the lead.

Mirror Mode

When you race in Mirror mode, each turn takes you in the opposite direction. Learn all of the described tactics, then flip them!

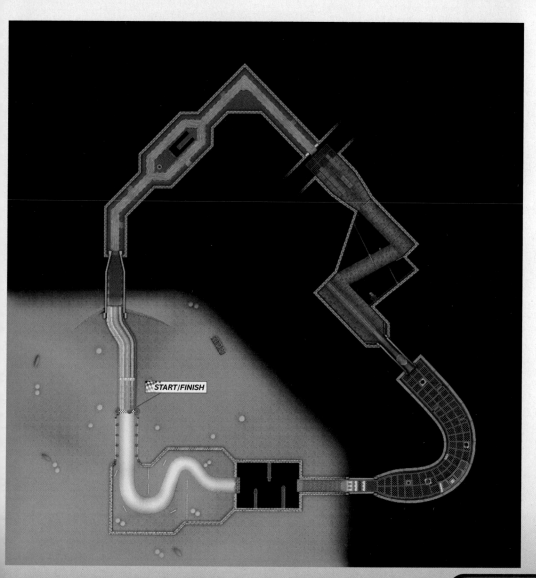

START/FINISH

Wario Shipyard

Star Cup

These wrecked ships make for a challenging course! Strong currents and aquatic creatures put your underwater driving to the test, but expect just as many hazards on the surface. Take advantage of the numerous dash panels, and use precision driving to cut a few corners on your way to the finish line.

ROAD HAZARDS

 MUD: These mud patches will slow you down. Use a Mushroom to speed across them, or steer your kart around them.

 STEEP DROPS: Don't slip into the mysterious depths; a fall will cost you valuable time.

 FISH BONES: As long as you stay out of their path, these nasty-looking characters are content to let you drive by.

 SIDESTEPPERS: You'll find these critters scuttling around the wrecked ships. Avoid crashing into them!

 ANCHORS: These swinging hazards pack quite a punch. If you're heading for a collision, make sure you change course.

 CURRENTS: These powerful currents can push you right off the track. If you have to drive through one, adjust your angle to compensate.

WRECKAGE: The shipyard is filled with the battered remains of countless vessels. Stay alert!

2   00:08.503

1   00:03.345

Drift through the first turn, then Mini-Turbo into the water. Drive up the incline and across the dash panel. Hop into the jump to gain a burst of speed when you splash back into the water. After you sink to the ground, make a hard drift to the right. As you come out of the curve, move to the middle of the path. Head up the ramp, then hop from the dash panel's edge. Drive straight over the next dash panel and into the tunnel. Drift along the track as it curves to the right.

10   00:44.001

Maintain your drift as you pass over the three dash panels. When you return to the main path, look for the small ramp along the next curve's inside edge. Once you're in position, release the drift to Super Mini-Turbo toward the ramp. Hop into the jump to cut across the gap, then speed your way to the end of the lap.

9   00:39.748

As you glide, take care to avoid the obstacles in your path. Aside from several masts, this area contains two swinging anchors. As you approach the water's edge, swoop up and land on the ledge to the left. Initiate a gentle drift, and follow the path as it curves to the right. The next shortcut is fairly risky, so make sure you're in control of your kart before you reach the dash panels.

8   00:34.548

Stay near the path's center and weave between the Sidesteppers. There's some wreckage to the left, so steer to the right if you're forced to swerve. Follow the dash panels through the narrow passage, then hop from the glide panel to barrel roll into a glide.

Time Trial

THE KART OF CHAMPIONS

 Character: Wario

 Kart: Bruiser

 Tires: Slim

 Glider: Beast Glider

③ 00:18.044

As you come out of the turn, release the drift to perform a Super Mini-Turbo. Pay attention to the pipe coming up on the right! Stay to the right if the current is active. If the water is calm, veer across the path's center.

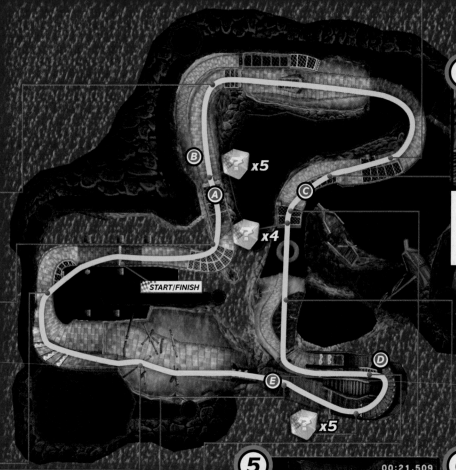

④ 00:19.879

You can save a little time by drifting along the path's edge, but watch out for the next current. If you start to slip over the edge, hop up to land on the track as it curves to the left.

TIP

If you're not feeling particularly daring, stick to the path's right side. It takes slightly longer, but it allows you to avoid this particular current.

⑤ 00:21.509

⑥ 00:24.343

⑦ 00:29.677

As you approach the ramp's end, make a hard drift to the right. Drop down to the main path and hold your drift through the turn. As the path straightens out, release the drift to boost down toward the small ramp. Hop into the jump and head back into the water.

Try to hold your drift through the curve. Mini-Turbo to the ramp's end and hop into the jump. As you pass over the large pipe, look for the patch of mud across the gap. When you land, use a Mushroom to boost through the mud—take care to avoid the masts! The track splits just past the anchor ahead of you. Aim for the path on the right. Slip past the anchor and follow the dash panels back to the surface.

TIP

The first anchor swings very slowly, so you shouldn't have much trouble slipping past it. If you're forced to veer left, however, don't fight it! The left path is only slightly longer, and it's much more important to avoid a collision.

MARIOKART 7

Tactics for Laps 2 and 3

Use the same basic tactics, but remember that this course has a lot of variables. Adjust your racing line to avoid Fish Bones, Sidesteppers, and swinging anchors.

Grand Prix

A

Make sure you hop each time you jump from a ramp. This provides a jump boost and ensures you can reach the higher item boxes.

B

If you need a few extra coins, check the curve just past the track's first jump. Veer to the left as you cross over the dash panel, then drive onto the track's banked section. This route takes a little longer, but there are a few dash panels to keep you from falling too far behind.

C

As you approach these item boxes, remember to account for the currents. If you're nudged out of position, you might wind up empty-handed. Of course, your main focus should be staying on the track!

D

If you take the left path past the first anchor, watch out for the hole in the deck. If you have a Banana, consider dropping it as you drift through this curve.

E

Bananas are particularly effective near the Sidesteppers. If you drop one here, the next racer will have a tough time getting through the area.

Mirror Mode

Master these tactics, then apply them to Mirror mode. Just flip each drift and turn!

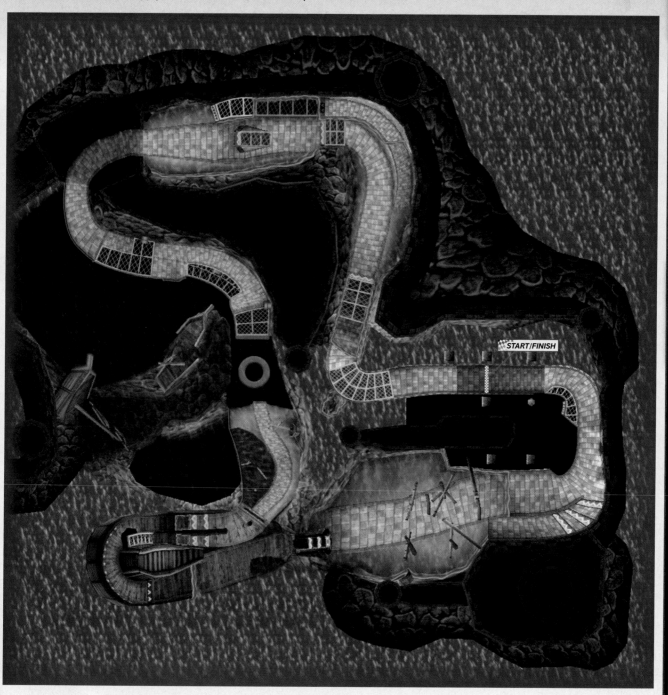

START/FINISH

Neo Bowser City

Star Cup

This course has only one route, so precision driving is the key to a fast completion time. Drift through every turn to gain as many Mini-Turbos and Super Mini-Turbos as possible. Unfortunately, the slick roads and unfenced turns make this easier said than done! There aren't many obstacles in your path, but the heavy rain has left a few rain puddles to slip up careless drivers. Keep your eyes peeled (and your kart on the track!) as you race through this futuristic city.

ROAD HAZARDS

 DARK BLUE TURF: Your kart slows down on dark blue turf. Stay off this surface or use a Mushroom to boost across it.

 STEEP DROPS: These dangerous locations are marked with red lights. Don't slip over the edge!

AIR VENTS: The air vents aren't particularly dangerous, but sudden gusts can jostle your kart.

PUDDLES: Driving through a puddle will cause your kart to spin out. These hazards can be hard to spot—stay alert!

1

As you approach the first curve, veer to the right, then drift back to the left. Start the drift early enough to charge a Mini-Turbo before the track curves back to the left. Release the drift, then start a new one as the track hooks back to the right. Super Mini-Turbo into the straightaway and follow the path into the tunnel.

7

As you exit the tunnel, aim for the coin in the center of the road. The first puddle is coming up on your left, so maintain your heading to ensure you avoid it. When the track starts to curve, begin a gentle drift to the left. After you pass the first puddle, move to the curve's inside edge.

CAUTION

As you glide through the end of each lap, avoid the sign above the finish line!

8

If you stay near the wall, you'll slip right past the remaining puddles. Hold your drift as the track loops around, then Super Mini-Turbo toward the glide panel. Hop into the jump, then glide your way to the end of the lap.

Time Trial

THE KART OF CHAMPIONS

Character: Metal Mario

Kart: Blue Seven

Tires: Monster

Glider: Paraglider

④ 00:14.981

The bridge is very narrow, so you don't have much room to drift. Try to charge a Mini-Turbo through each curve, but focus on avoiding the guardrails.

③ 00:07.905

② 00:06.445

As you approach the next corner, make a hard drift to the left. Use a Mushroom to boost across the blue turf, then release the drift as you return to the asphalt. Watch out for the large pillar protruding from the wall! Veer to the left, then head straight out of the tunnel. Drift through the next curve, then Super Mini-Turbo onto the covered bridge.

⑤ 00:21.647

As you exit the covered bridge, look for the red lights on your left. These lights indicate a steep drop, so use caution whenever you see them. As you drift through the next two turns, try to stay near the track's center.

⑥ 00:29.344

When the track pulls away from the wall, things get a little more dangerous. Drift through the coins along the curve's inside edge, but be careful not to slip off. When you come out of the turn, Super Mini-Boost toward the tunnel ahead of you.

MARIOKART7

Tactics for Laps 2 and 3

Use the exact same tactics to complete the remaining laps. Be particularly careful around the rain puddles. Now that you've collected the nearby coins, you might have a little more trouble recognizing these hazards.

Grand Prix

With its blind turns and enclosed areas, this track has plenty of great areas to use items. Drop a Banana as you drift through a turn, or send a Green Shell ricochetting off of walls and guardrails. Be careful around the air vents; they're fairly harmless on their own, but a sudden gust can nudge you onto an item you intend to avoid.

Look for opportunities to draft behind leading opponents. The narrow track makes this technique fairly easy to employ. As always, use the Touch Screen to check for any unequipped items your target might be holding.

The covered bridge is an ideal location to use your items. If possible, drop a Banana in the center of the track, or toss a Green Shell behind you.

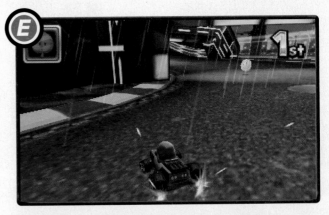

It's extremely dangerous to jostle through the unfenced turns. Even heavier racers should consider halting attacks until reaching the straightaways. However, if you have a suitable item, this is another great spot to trip up nearby opponents.

As you drift past the rain puddles, try to leave a Banana near the curve's inside edge. If you can force your opponents to take a wide turn, you should be able to improve your lead as you dash for the finish line.

Mirror Mode

As long as you take each turn in the opposite direction, you can use the same tactics to dominate this flipped track!

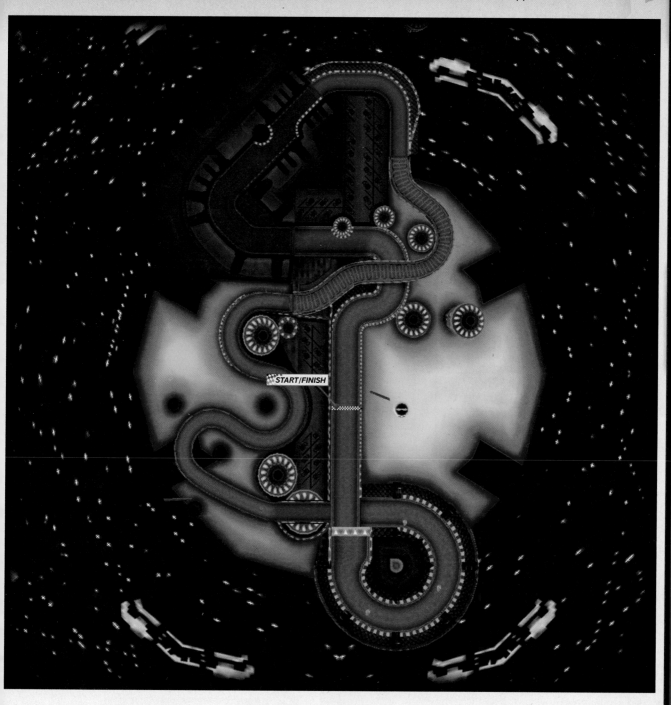

START/FINISH

Maka Wuhu

Star Cup

Drift, boost, and glide your way through a single lap of this winding course. Hop from every bump and ramp you cross, and look for chances to boost through the off-road shortcuts. Loop your way up the mountain, then glide down to the finish line. You'll encounter plenty of hazards on this wild course, and most of them involve rough terrain. Keep your speed up and watch those drifts!

ROAD HAZARDS

 GRASS AND SAND: When in doubt, stay on the track. Without a Mushroom, a detour across these low-traction surfaces will cost you valuable time.

 MUD: You won't lose much speed near the edge of a mud patch, but the deeper you go, the more your kart will struggle.

 STEEP DROPS: There are plenty of dangerous falls along this track. A sudden slip can cost you the lead!

 BOULDERS: Dodge these rolling rocks or risk a crushing defeat. Watch the mountain roads for these big boulders.

6 — 00:48.366

7 — 00:52.959

When you exit the tunnel, look for the traffic cones coming up on the right. Part of the track has crumbled away, so stay to the left. As you pass by the traffic cones, make a gentle drift to the left. Watch for the upcoming patch of grass. When you spot it, use a Mushroom to boost off the track. Steer your kart through the gap between the mountainside and the moss-covered rock. Drop down into the small lake, then follow the path back up to the track.

8 — 00:59.354

If you wish, use your last Mushroom to cut through the small castle near the end of section 2. However, this shortcut's sharp bends and grassy exit make it less than ideal. Instead, consider following the track as it curves around the castle. Drift through the turn to charge a Super Mini-Turbo, then use your Mushroom toward the end of the race!

TIP

There are two bubbling fissures at the bottom of the lake. If you're properly aligned, jump boost off of the fissure on the left. If your kart lands at an angle, it's safer to simply drive past it.

CAUTION

Veer left as you exit the water—if you don't, you're likely to drive right off the course!

4 — 00:29.099
2/3

As you enter section 2, use a Mushroom to cut across the grass on your left. Veer to the left as you enter the tunnel; the next stretch is dangerous, so make sure your kart is under control.

3 — 00:24.097

As the track curves to the right, try to drift along the path's center. Try to avoid the surrounding mud puddles, but don't worry if you make contact. As long as you hold the drift, you can cross over the mud without losing much speed. As you come out of the curve, release the drift to Super Mini-Turbo to the end of section 1.

Time Trial

THE KART OF CHAMPIONS

Character: Yoshi

Kart: Standard

Tires: Monster

Glider: Super Glider

⑨ 00:41.917

When you enter section 3, drift along the path as it curves around the mountain. Watch out for the boulders coming around the bend! As you exit the curve, Super Mini-Turbo into the straightaway. When the track takes you back down the mountain, drift along the track's right side. Follow the road to the glide panel, then hop into the jump for an additional burst of speed.

⑤ 00:29.099

As the tunnel walls pull away from the track, try to stay near the path's center! Hop each time you cross over a bump, and use the dash panels to jump over gaps in the track. Drift through each curve, but make sure you don't slip over the edge.

SECTION 3

?x5

?x5

?x5

C

B

SECTION 2

?x2

?x2

A

?x5

D

?x2

START

FINISH

⑩ 01:32.255

As you glide, aim for the target on the floating platform. After you touch down, continue across the next glide panel and glide straight down to the path ahead of you. If you still have a Mushroom, use it when you land. Boost through the rock formation and across the finish line.

② 00:16.754

① 00:03.998

After you pass the first mud puddle, look for the ramp coming up on the left. Hop along the remaining bumps, then veer onto the ramp and jump over to the narrow strip of dirt. When you land, follow the path back to the track.

The first stretch doesn't offer many chances to drift. Stay near the track's center to pass over each of the ramps along the path. Make sure you hop into every jump; the small boosts can really add up. When you hit the fourth ramp, use the dash panel to jump through the coins above the parked vehicle. Veer to the left as soon as you land. There's a small path to the right, but stick to the main road. Hop as you drive across each bump to maximize your speed through the curve.

INTRODUCTION

NEW CUPS

CLASSIC CUPS

BATTLE MAPS

Grand Prix

Plan your attacks carefully! This course has several possible routes, and you won't gain much by laying a trap on a deserted path. Make sure you have a possible target before you use an item.

As always, be careful near steep drops. Reckless jostling is just as dangerous for you as it is for your opponent! Equip items to defend yourself, or keep your distance from the other racers.

If your opponents have a knack for interrupting your drifts, look for new opportunities to jump boost. The track is full of bumps and ramps; keep your eyes open!

If you're lagging behind as you glide toward the finish line, grab an item box from one of the floating platforms; a last-minute Red Shell or Mushroom might give you the edge you need!

Mirror Mode

This course has all of the same shortcuts, but every turn has been flipped. With a little adjustment, you can use the same tactics and claim victory in Mirror mode!

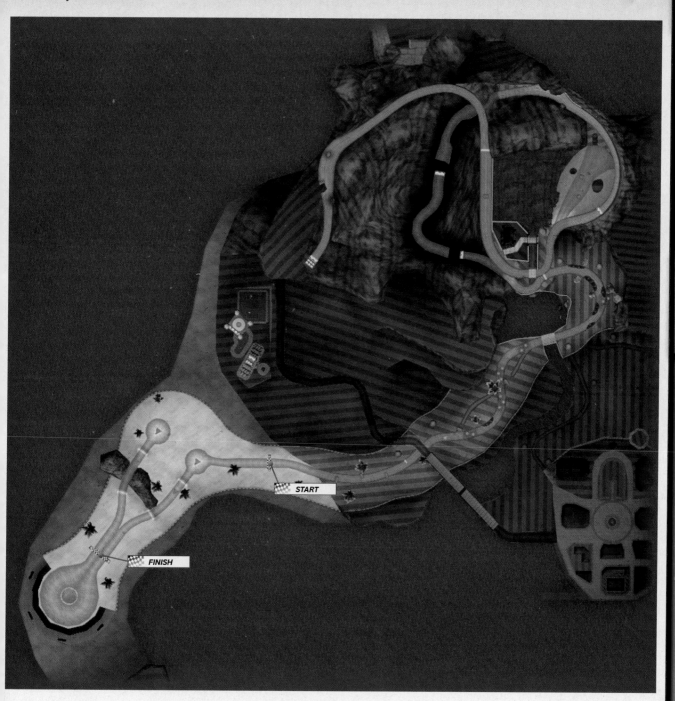

DK Jungle

This jungle course has enough twists, turns, and jumps to test even the most skilled racers. Dodge the mud puddles and wildlife, or use the hidden glide panel to soar above the competition. The ancient temple has some extremely dangerous turns, but a few well-timed drifts should help you speed right through the area. This wild setting has its share of hazards. Stay focused!

ROAD HAZARDS

 GRASS: Keep your kart off the grass; the jungle foliage will only slow you down.

 MUD: The longer you stay in the mud, the more speed you lose. Try to avoid this low-traction surface!

 STEEP DROPS: Sheer cliffs and crumbling ruins make for some dangerous turns. Stay in control to avoid nasty falls.

 DK BARRELS: Steer clear of these giant barrels; they're sturdy enough to stop your kart cold.

 FROGOON: You'll find these critters hopping around the unpaved roads. You'll spin out if you hit one, so take care to avoid them.

 TIKI GOONS: Tiki Goons wander across the track, trying to trip up careless racers. Avoid these slow-moving enemies.

 SCREAMING PILLAR: These Screaming Pillars can push your glider off course. If you see a shaking Screaming Pillar, stay away from its mouth!

③ `00:11.582`

Drift along the track's left edge, but watch out for the wandering Tiki Goons. These enemies move fairly slowly, so you shouldn't have much trouble slipping past each of them. Try to hold your drift through the curve, then Super Mini-Turbo across the bridge.

④ `01:05.650`

TIP

Depending on your chosen kart configuration, this drift can be very difficult. Experiment with various approach angles to find one that works. It's much easier to get through the next area if your glider is deployed. Keep practicing until you get it!

Drift through the right turn after the bridge, then look for the ramp off the track's left edge. Veer to the right, then make a hard drift back toward the ramp. To use this shortcut, you must drift through the mud and across the planks, then follow the ramp up to a glide panel. If you succeed, jump from the ramp's end to barrel roll into your glide. If you miss the turn (or fall off the ramp), use a Mushroom to recover from the attempt.

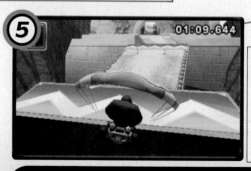

⑤ `01:09.644`

If you managed to reach the glide panel, use the three dash panels along the main path to extend your glide; touch down on each one to keep your glider deployed all the way to the temple entrance.

CAUTION

If your glider isn't active, mind your angle as you drive across each platform! Make sure your kart is aimed straight at the next platform to avoid costly falls.

Time Trial

THE KART OF CHAMPIONS

DK Character: Donkey Kong

Kart: Standard

Tires: Wood

Glider: Swooper

2 00:05.035

After the second turn, the track splits to flank two large trees. The paths are nearly identical, so you can take either of them. As you drive over the exposed root, hop up to gain a jump boost. Drive onto the dash panel, hop from the edge, then hop again as you bounce off the giant flower. The next strip of track is fairly narrow, so make sure you make a clean landing after each jump.

1 00:02.112

As you drift through the first curve, avoid the DK Barrel along the track's right edge. Drift gently until you pass it, then make a hard right turn to avoid sliding off the track. As you come out of the curve, release the drift and start a new one to the left.

B

? x4

? x4

A

START/FINISH

C

D

? x2

? x2

8 00:42.036

When you land, make a hard drift through the first left turn. The path is fairly narrow, so make sure you don't slide over the edge. As you come out of the curve, release the drift to Mini-Turbo toward the incline at the path's end. Hop into the jump, then use the burst of speed to race through the end of the lap.

6 00:31.634

Drift through the turns inside the temple, but keep the kart on the track! If you haven't already used a Mushroom, consider doing so through the first left turn. Hold your drift through the next corner, then Super Mini-Turbo toward the exit.

7 00:36.847

Hop from the glide panel at the temple exit, then glide between the Screaming Pillars. If one of the Screaming Pillar starts to shake, veer away to avoid the impending scream.

Tactics for Laps 2 and 3

Use the same basic tactics to complete the remaining laps. Adjust your racing line to avoid Tiki Goons and Frogoons as they move across the track. The shortest route through the course bypasses many of the available coins, so make sure you grab each one that crosses your path!

Grand Prix

Item boxes are few and far between, so do your best to grab one from the first group. If you can't jostle your way to the head of the pack, consider hanging back just enough to see which item boxes your opponents hit. If you do this, make sure you drift through the curve—the Super Mini-Turbo will keep you from falling too far behind.

As you drive through the Tiki Goons, use the Touch Screen to keep an eye on the other racers. The slightest jostle could send you into an enemy or off the course. This is a great spot to draft behind your opponents, but expect trailing racers to use the same tactic.

If you have a Banana handy, try to place it near one of the course's big drops. These items can be extremely effective on the platforms that lead to the temple.

Don't forget to grab those coins! As effective as the shortcuts are, they can make it difficult to reach the 10-coin limit. Consider sacrificing an early lead to collect your coins, then try your best to hang on to them as you push your way into the lead.

Mirror Mode

Use the same big drifts and great shortcuts in Mirror mode, but don't forget to take each turn in the opposite direction!

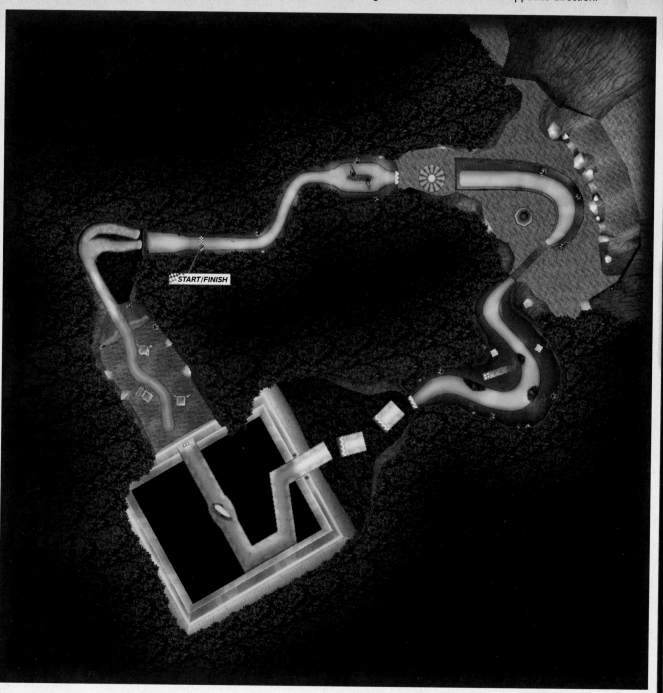

START/FINISH

Rosalina's Ice World

Special Cup

To claim victory on this wintry course, you must plan each drift carefully. Use the banked turns to maintain your speed, but don't let your kart creep too high up the walls. The frozen pond is starting to thaw; if the ice doesn't suit you, consider heading into the water. Use the dash panels inside the cavern, but make sure you stay in control of your kart!

ROAD HAZARDS

SNOW: The ice can be hard to manage, but it's a better option than the snow! Your kart slows down considerably if you drive onto this low-traction surface.

STEEP DROPS: This course has its share of nasty drops. To stay in the lead, you'll have to stay on the track.

PENGUINS: Look for these plucky penguins waddling across the ice or swimming in the water. Steer around them to avoid a spinout.

ICICLES: Steer clear of these giant icicles. They're not very sturdy, but you'll stop if you hit one.

④ 00:17.401

After you grab the coin, veer back to the track's center. Drive over the ramp and hop into a jump. When you land, steer around the hole in the ice ahead of you. You can veer in either direction, but consider the waddling penguins when you choose a path. There are a few smaller holes just ahead, so try to maneuver your kart between them.

⑤ 00:23.738

Use a couple of small drifts to stay on the narrow strip of ice. You should be able to hold each drift long enough to charge a Mini-Turbo. You're heading for the cavern just ahead of you. If you fall into the water, drive to the pond's end and return to the path.

⑥ 00:30.709

As you enter the cavern, look for the coin near the left wall. As the path curves to the right, veer toward the left wall and drive through the coin. After you grab it, make a hard drift to the left. Try to slip between the two icicles ahead of you. Grab the coin near the icicles, then release the drift to Mini-Turbo through the turn.

CAUTION

This drift can be very effective, but it doesn't leave much room for error. Take care to avoid crashing through the icicles or into the wall.

Time Trial

THE KART OF CHAMPiONS

Character: Rosalina

Kart: Zucchini

Tires: Red Monster

Glider: Super Glider

2   00:08.710

When you pass under the arch, release the drift and Mini-Turbo toward the wall on your left. As the track loops to the right, drift along the banked wall to avoid slipping off the ice.

3   01:01.905

Hold the drift through the end of the loop, then start a new drift as the track bends to the left. The boost of speed from the resulting Super Mini-Turbo might force you onto the wall on the right; drift back to the path's center, but make sure your angle is gentle enough to maintain control. Aim your kart at the coin coming up on the left, then release the drift to Mini-Turbo toward it.

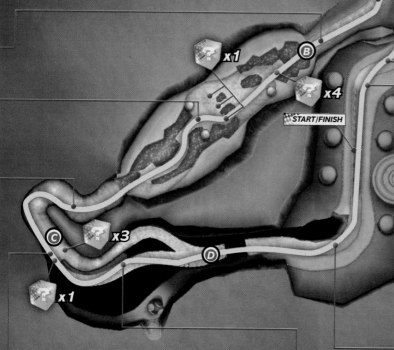

A

B

x1

x4

START/FINISH

x4

C

x3

D

x1

1   00:02.346

Drift through the first curve to charge a Mini-Turbo, then release the drift and start a new one to the left. Try to stay off the banked wall to the right of the arch.

9   01:29.543

Hop into the jump as you exit the cavern, then follow the track as it curves to the left. Drift through the turn, but take care to stay on the track. When you come out of the curve, Super Mini-Turbo toward the end of the lap.

7   00:35.109

8   01:22.781

Drive along the path's right side, and look for the dash panel at the track's edge. Be very careful during your approach! Move your kart to the track's edge and begin a hard drift to the left. Hold the drift across the dash panel, then move toward the track's left edge. There are two gentle curves ahead of you, and each of them has a dash panel along its outside edge. Start a fresh drift between each dash panel to stay on the track as you speed through the curve.

Tactics for Laps 2 and 3

`01:05.206`

After you complete the first lap, a section of the ice is removed from the pond. Use a Mushroom to boost over the larger gap on each of the remaining laps. The third Mushroom can be used at any time, but consider saving it to recover from a collision or an unplanned swim. Other than that, you can use the same basic tactics to complete the event.

Grand Prix

A

The large loop near the start of each lap is a great place to draft behind other racers. Trailing opponents are bound to try this as well, so be ready to dodge any karts that might boost past you. This is also an ideal location to drop a Banana.

B

Even without a Mushroom, you can clear the large gap that appears in the pond. Drive straight across the ramp's center, then hop into the jump. Note that a mistimed jump can send you crashing into the ice. If you'd rather not risk it, drive straight into the water. This path contains some item boxes, coins, and several bumps from which you can jump boost.

C

The dash panels in the cavern are much harder to negotiate when opponents are nearby. In this case, consider following the path to the left. It's a bit slower, but you'll find it much easier to endure frequent jostling.

D

The cavern exit is another great place to use suitable items. As trailing opponents funnel in from both sides, you stand an excellent chance of hitting someone with a Green Shell or a well-placed Banana.

Mirror Mode

This snowscape is just as striking in Mirror mode. Use all of the same tactics, but flip the direction of each turn.

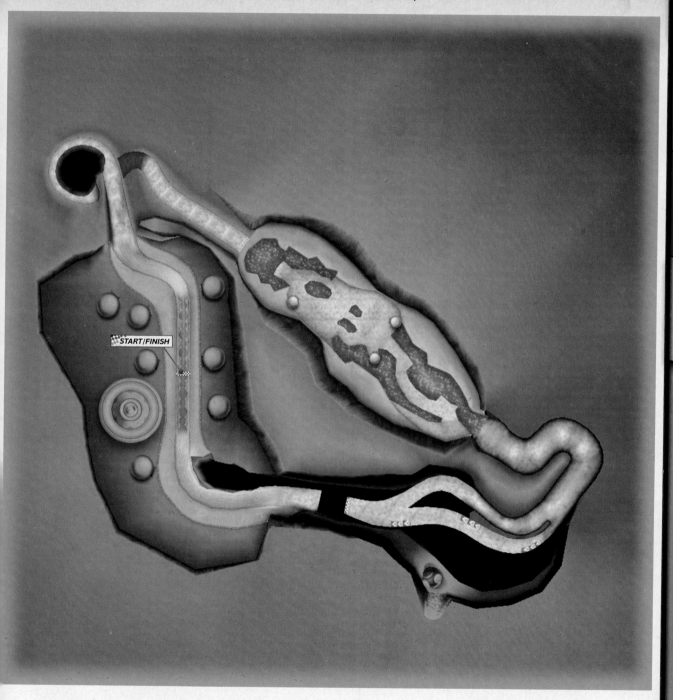

START/FINISH

Bowser's Castle

Special Cup

This course may not be the most inviting setting, but it has a few shortcuts to help you speed through the area. Drifting is as important as ever, but a few conveniently located ramps allow for some time-saving jumps. Stay on course (and out of the lava) as you race through Bowser's Castle!

ROAD HAZARDS

 DIRT: Driving on this loose dirt slows you down. Keep your kart off of unpaved surfaces.

 LAVA: Much of the track runs above pools of lava. Even a short fall can end in disaster!

 LAVA PLUMES: Watch out for the lava that spurts up from the track. The course's smaller ramps tend to lead you over these hazards. Don't get caught in a sudden eruption!

 LAVA STREAMS: There are several giant vats pouring lava onto the track. Driving through one of these streams will cause you to spin out.

 THWOMPS: Watch out for these heavy hitters! Avoid Thwomps as they slam down to the track.

⑤

00:21.500

After you exit the tunnel, hop onto the large paddle wheel. The paddle wheel is spinning, so adjust your angle to avoid falling off. Drive through one of the gaps between the paddles and drop into the water.

⑥

00:25.260

The path curves to the right just after you land, so start your drift immediately. Aim for the gap between the first two lava streams, then release the drift to Mini-Turbo toward it. As you pass the lava stream on your right, initiate a drift to the left.

⑦

00:27.787

Drift around the second lava stream and move toward the curve's inside edge. Line your kart up with the dash panel ahead of you. Try to grab the coin at the ramp's top, but make sure you're lined up for a proper jump. You want to pass just to the right of the last lava stream—you don't have much room to land, so a proper approach is crucial. Remember to hop into the jump!

⑧

00:32.597

Follow the path out of the water, and look for the small ramp coming up on the left. The nearby lava plume might prevent you from collecting the coin, but you can safely perform a jump boost if you stay near the ramp's edge. When you land, stay near the track's right edge and drift through the curve.

Time Trial

THE KART OF CHAMPIONS

- **Character:** Bowser
- **Kart:** Bruiser
- **Tires:** Red Monster
- **Glider:** Super Glider

CAUTION

At top speed, you can drift right across the small gaps in the shortcut. At lower speeds, however, this technique is much less reliable!

4 00:18.266

The second Thwomp is at the hall's end. Stay near the path's center as you approach the Thwomp, and look for the ramp coming up on your left. Drift onto the ramp, then Mini-Turbo through the coins in front of you.

3 00:13.785

As you turn the corner, hold the drift to line your kart up with the ramp near the left wall. There are two lava plumes that erupt just past the ramp. The one nearest the wall should appear as you approach, so veer slightly to the right before you release your drift. Drive across the ramp, and hop into the jump for an additional boost when you land. Dodge around the first Thwomp, then make a hard drift through the right turn.

? x4

? x2

B

? x2

? x4

E

? x5

START/FINISH

A

C

D

2 00:07.521

The track splits on the lower level; veer toward either path as you drop through the hole. Take care to stay on the track as you drive over the dash panel! When the boost wears off, make a hard drift to the left and follow the spiral staircase around the curve. Try to stay near the wall on your left until you reach the top of the stairs.

1 00:03.952

There's a glide panel at the start of the lap. Hop into the jump for an extra burst of speed, then glide straight for the castle entrance. Touch down on the upper level, then follow the path inside.

9 00:38.161

10 00:39.162

The upcoming shortcut is risky, but it's well worth taking! As you come out of the curve, move to the path's center, then veer back to the right. There's a ramp just ahead of you and another ramp across the lava. Line your kart up with both ramps, then use a Mushroom to boost between the ramps and back up to the track. Hop from the top of each ramp to help ensure you clear both gaps. When you land on the track, make a hard drift to the right to avoid falling off. Follow the path around the curve and across the glide panel, then glide through the end of the lap.

Tactics for Laps 2 and 3

After you complete the first lap, glide over to one of the platforms on either side of the track. Grab the coins from the platform, then use one of the dash panels to jump to the castle entrance. On lap 3, collect the coins from the other platform.

Use the same basic tactics, but adjust your racing line to avoid the Thwomps and lava plumes as needed.

Bananas work well almost anywhere on the track, but the spiral stairs offer the best place to use a Green Shell. Toss one behind you to create a serious hazard for nearby opponents!

Grand Prix

You shouldn't have any trouble the first time you glide to the castle, but this area can be much more dangerous later in the race. Since powerful items can knock you out of the sky, move to one of the platforms as quickly as possible.

Remember that you need a lot of speed to drift through the first shortcut. If your opponents have slowed you down, hop across the gap or stick to the main path.

Try jostling troublesome racers off the track or into one of the lava streams—just remember to avoid picking fights with heavier racers!

If your opponents favor the upper entrance, consider entering the castle from below. This can often be your best shot at an early item box.

Mirror Mode

Use the same tactics to drift, jump, and glide your way through the finish line. Simply flip each turn you've learned to master this track in Mirror mode.

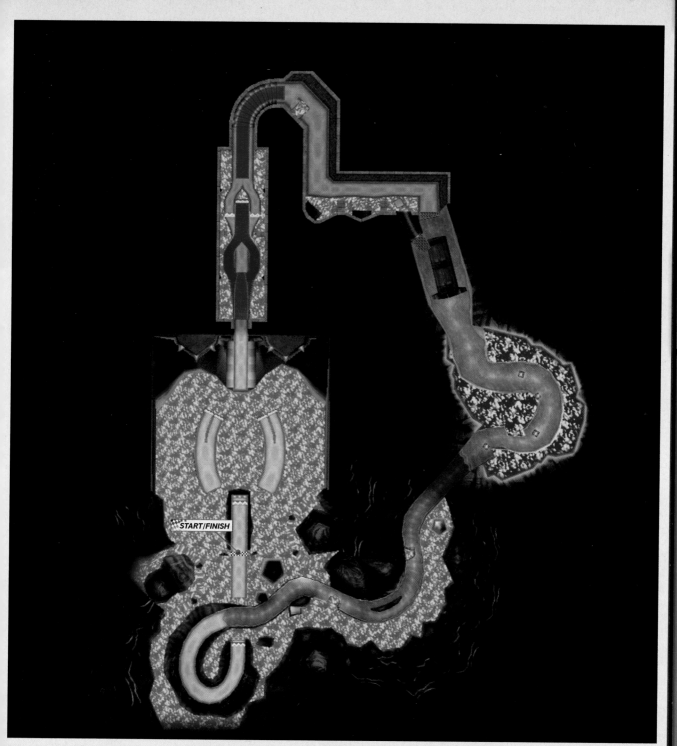

START/FINISH

Rainbow Road

Special Cup

As you might have guessed, Rainbow Road is one of the game's most challenging tracks. Drift, jump, and glide your way through a single lap of perilous turns and disorienting angles. Most of the track is completely unfenced, so it takes a lot of skill to stay in the race. Don't be afraid to use the breaks in an emergency—it's better to slow down than to suffer a costly fall. You won't find many shortcuts here, but there are plenty of dash panels to help you along the way.

ROAD HAZARDS

 STEEP DROPS: You're in near-constant danger of falling off the track. Keep your jumps true and your drifts in check!

 CHOMPS: Keep your distance from these massive Chomps! You'll find a few of them near the end of section 2.

 ASTEROIDS: If you manage to glide through section 3, make sure you avoid these floating hazards.

Just after the loop, the track curves back to the left. Use a drift to stay near the path's center, but straighten yourself out before you reach the next dash panel. Hop into the jump, then hop again when you bounce off the platform. If you hit the dash panel head-on, you should land safely on the next strip of track. Make a hard drift through the turn, then Super Mini-Turbo into the straightaway. Stay near the path's center to collect a few more coins on your way to section 2.

After the first dash panel, the track is broken into short segments. As you approach each dash panel, carefully aim your kart toward the next segment. Try to collect at least one of the coins from each segment, but focus on landing clean jumps. Remember to hop from the edge of each dash panel. When the track loops to the right, drift into the curve. Hold the drift through the entire loop as you drop down along the remaining segments.

To earn a fast completion time, you'll have to make the most of every turn. The track's first curve has a fence along its outside edge, but you won't find many more along this course. As you drift through each curve, try to stay near the track's center. You won't always be able to do so, but the effort should help you maintain control of your kart.

10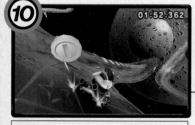

The final stretch contains one of the course's most dangerous curves. If you still have a Mushroom, use it to boost up the steep incline. Drift through the coins in the track's center, then Super Mini-Turbo out of the turn. The last curve's outside edge is protected by a fence, so try not to hit it as you start your next drift. Release the drift as you come out of the turn, then Super Mini-Turbo toward the finish line.

9

As you exit the tube, veer to the left and pass through the golden ring. Touch down on the ramp ahead of you, then use the dash panels to speed under the asteroids. The track narrows shortly after each ramp, so aim your jumps accordingly.

8

As you drive along the tube, take advantage of any dash panels that move into your path. Pay close attention to the dash panels lining the exit. As you approach, veer onto the nearest glide panel to deploy your glider.

Time Trial

THE KART OF CHAMPIONS

 Character: Honey Queen

 Kart: Bumble V

Tires: Standard

Glider: Flower Glider

TIP
On this track, your Mushrooms are best used to recover from collisions. If you can't avoid hitting the fence, use a Mushroom to get back up to speed.

5 00:53.392

Hop from the glide panel at the track's end, then glide down to the planetary ring. After you land, drift through the curve. Try to hold the drift along the entire ring, but mind the gaps on either side of you. When you reach the dash panels, stay near the path's center to pass over each of them. When you spot the glide panel, straighten your kart and release the drift to perform a Super Mini-Turbo. Hop from the glide panel, then glide through the golden ring for an extra burst of speed.

4 00:38.250

Section 2 starts with a very sharp banked turn. Make a hard drift to the right, and try to stay near the curve's inside edge. As you exit the curve, your kart should slide onto the banked section. Steer hard to the left and release the drift. Try to use the Super Mini-Turbo to ease your way down from the banked section. If your kart slides down too quickly, you're likely to slam into the fence on your right.

? x1 **SECTION 2**

? x5

? x1

A

? x5

B

? x1 **?** x3

C

? x4 **?** x1

 START/FINISH

? x1

? x4 **?** x5

D

6 01:05.122

SECTION 3

7 01:22.821

Glide down to the banked turns, then carefully drift through each of them. Stay near the track's center, and try to pass over the edge of each dash panel. When you reach the straightaway, the track begins to ripple. As each wave passes under you, hop up to gain a jump boost. Avoid the holes along the path, then drop down from the end of the track.

NOTE
Some of the dash panels in section 3 look a little different from what you're used to seeing. They provide the same great boost, however, so make sure you use them!

Even with the bouncing Chomps, the end of section 2 is one of Rainbow Road's safest areas. Jump boost off of each crater in your path, and consider using a Mushroom on your way into section 3. Drive along the dash panels near the track's center, then head into the spinning tube.

Don't shy away from the item boxes at the end of section 2. If you're lagging behind at this point, a powerful item is your best chance to get back in the race.

If you exit the tube without hitting a glide panel, you can still get through the area very quickly. Take advantage of the dash panels and golden rings on your way into the last stretch. Boost past nearby opponents for a chance to jostle them off the track, and try to gain some ground as you drift through the final turns.

Grand Prix

Jostling is a very risky tactic on this track, but you may not always have a choice. If a larger opponent is determined to crash into you, slow down just enough the let them pass, then try to draft behind them. The resulting boost might be enough to knock them off the track. If you choose to initiate a jostle, choose your target wisely. Picking a fight with an evenly matched racer may do nothing more than slow both of you down.

A Banana works well in any unfenced turn, but consider dropping them near dash panels. These tempting targets are difficult to resist, and overeager opponents are likely to hit them.

Mirror Mode

As if these turns weren't hard enough to master on the standard course! Luckily, the same tactics apply when you race along this flipped track.

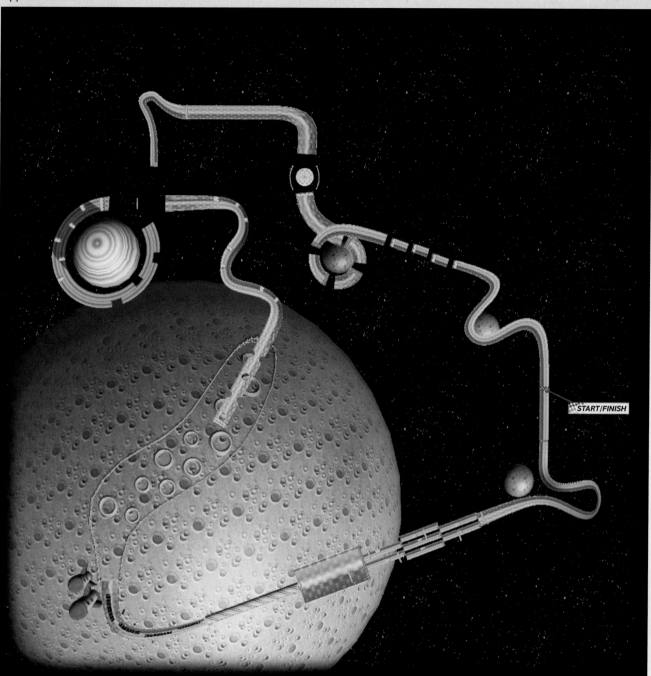

START/FINISH

N64 Luigi Raceway

Shell Cup

This simple track requires a smooth racing line for maximum speed. Drift along the inside of each curve, then Super Mini-Turbo into every straightaway. There aren't many shortcuts to speak of, but you can cut a few corners if you have some Mushrooms to spare.

ROAD HAZARDS

GRASS AND SAND: Stay on the track and you'll be fine! Driving across grass or sand slows your kart. You can use a Mushroom to boost across them, but it's generally best to stick to the pavement.

③ As you enter the tunnel, drift to the right to get a small boost. Try to stay close to the right wall when doing this. Avoid hitting the wall at all costs, as it will slow you down dramatically.

④ As you come out of the tunnel, drift to the right to get another small boost. Do this quickly to avoid going into the dirt off the track. If you do go into the dirt, get back on the main road right away!

⑤ As soon as you receive a small boost from your previous drift, hop and drift to the left and stay along the inside portion of the track. While drifting, collect the coins that are closest to the inside of the track.

Time Trial

THE KART OF CHAMPIONS

 Character: Luigi

 Kart: Pipe Frame

 Tires: Slick

 Glider: Paraglider

2 · 00:12.022

As you head into the first bend in the track, drift to the left while trying to stay as close to the track's edge as possible. As you drift all the way around this bend, try to grab the coins that are the closest to the inside of the track.

1 · 00:03.994

Shortly after you rocket start off the starting line, you'll see a large bump in the road ahead of you. Hop off of this bump to get a much-needed small boost.

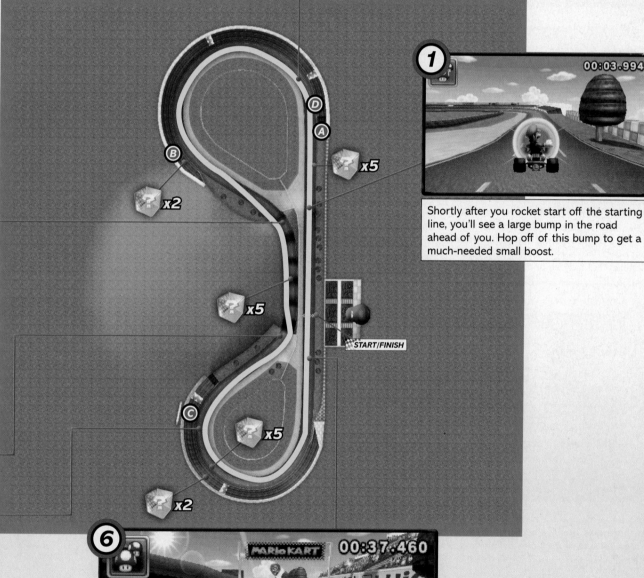

When your boost from the previous drift ends, use a Mushroom to keep your speed up along the straightaway. This will complete your first lap.

6 · 00:37.460

INTRODUCTION

NEW CUPS

CLASSIC CUPS

BATTLE MAPS

Tactics for Laps 2 and 3

Use the same basic tactics to complete the remaining laps. Adjust your racing line if you need to collect more coins; otherwise, use your remaining Mushrooms to cut across the grass and sand along the inside of the track's large curves. Make sure you're drifting while you do this!

Grand Prix

If the main track is crowded at the beginning, you can drive onto the blue section of the raised track just to the right of the first bend. This section of the track is also great for avoiding Bananas that may be on the main track.

As you go along the blue section of track, collect all the coins. At the end of the blue section of track, there are two item boxes; be sure to grab one before dropping back down onto the main track.

After coming out of the tunnel, you'll see another blue section of track to the right. Feel free to take this route if the main raceway is too crowded or if there are Bananas to avoid!

As you finish your first lap, you may see the Luigi hot-air balloon swooping down toward the track. There may be a bonus item box hanging from the bottom of it, so make sure to grab it if you come across it.

Mirror Mode

You'll hardly notice the difference when this track is flipped! Just follow the big turns to the right instead of the left.

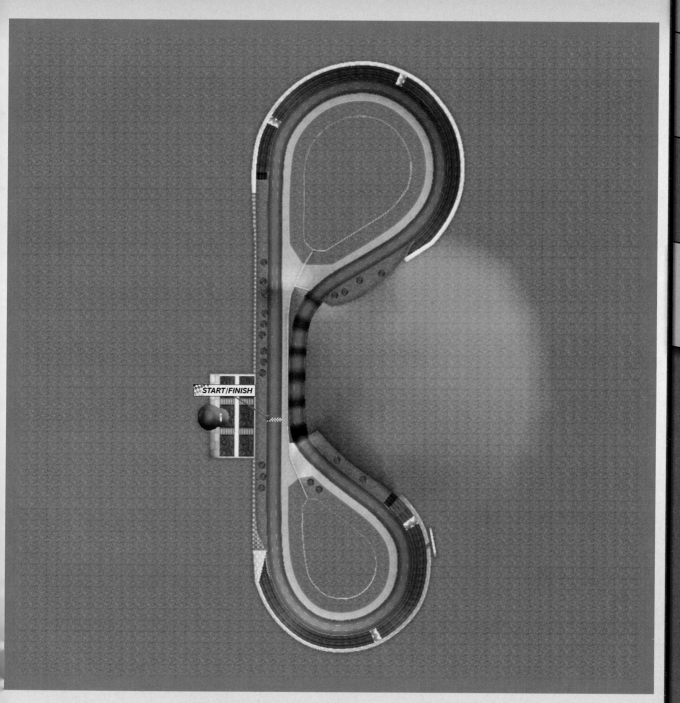

GBA Bowser Castle 1

Shell Cup

This track is filled with sharp turns, angry Thwomps, and plenty of lava. Drift through patches of sand and gravel when you can't find a route around them, and keep an eye out for leaping Lava Bubbles. Between the dash panels along the course and the small boosts from your drifts, you should finish this track in no time!

ROAD HAZARDS

SAND: Your kart slows down if you drive across these sand patches. When you can't avoid crossing one, drift through it to maintain your speed.

GRAVEL: Keep your tires away from this loose gravel! You lose a lot of speed if you drive across it. As with the sand, you can drift across gravel to minimize the slowing effect.

LAVA: Stay out of the lava! A slip off the track will cost you valuable time.

THWOMPS: Don't let these Thwomps get the drop on you! These stony creatures slam down to the track with surprising speed.

LAVA BUBBLES: Each time you jump across a gap, keep an eye out for these Lava Bubbles. Don't get caught in a midair collision.

When approaching the two Thwomps, begin a drift to go right between them. Hold this drift around the next corner and continue holding it until you see the next straightaway.

When you hit this straightaway, keep holding your drift while using one of your Mushrooms for a speed boost. This will help speed you through this hazardous area with Thwomps and portions of the gravel on the track that slow you down.

Right before the straightaway ends, when you see the Thwomps, release your drift for a speed boost. As soon as you release the drift, begin a drift to the left and go right between the Thwomps while collecting the coins around them. Hold the drift until you reach the next straightaway, and release it right before reaching the dash panel ahead of you.

Time Trial

THE KART OF CHAMPIONS

Character: Bowser

Kart: Koopa Clown

Tires: Roller

Glider: Super Glider

1

Right after doing a rocket start, drift to the left and stay very close to the wall. Hold this drift around the turn and collect the coins ahead.

2

Release your previous drift you were holding to cut the corner of the next turn. You'll speed boost right over the lava! Make sure you're not too far out from the corner, though, or you'll fall directly into the lava, losing all of your Mushrooms for boosting, along with valuable seconds off the clock.

TIP

There is a ramp to the left in the lava that you can access during laps 2 and 3 after the glide panel rises. Try and use it to see if you can shave even more time off your lap!

7

Drift as soon as you go through the long straightaway. The finish line is ahead of you. Alternate drifting left and right while going around the bends in this last stretch, and try to get Mini-Turbos if possible. Just make sure you don't hit the walls!

6

As you go through the dash panels along the straightaway, hop as you cross over each one for a speed boost. This will help you get down this long straightaway much quicker.

Tactics for Laps 2 and 3

After you complete the first lap, a ramp appears near the Lava Bubbles. Use its glide panel to glide through the area. Beyond this change, use the same tactics to complete the remaining laps.

Grand Prix

A

During your second and third laps, take the ramp with the glide panel to soar above your opponents, and avoid getting hit by potential Lava Bubbles.

B

Try to place Bananas around the sand pits near the finish line to force your opponents to go through the slower terrain.

C

Drifting through sand pits that normally slow you down is a great way to keep your speed up. Using Mushrooms for a speed boost through them is also a valid tactic.

D

Avoid hitting the Thwomps on the track—they'll stop you immediately. It can be risky driving under one when it is up in the air. If you drive under a shadow, there is a good chance you'll get flattened!

Mirror Mode

Use all of the same tactics to stay on the track, but make sure you take each corner in the opposite direction!

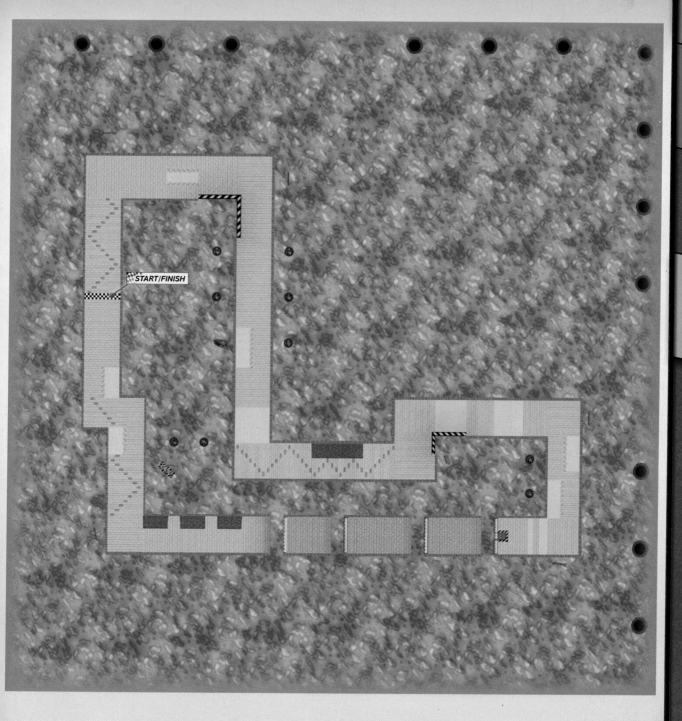

START/FINISH

Wii Mushroom Gorge

Shell Cup

Don't get carried away as you bounce through this colorful course; it's a long way down to the bottom of Mushroom Gorge. Remember to hop each time you bounce! Those jump boosts add up over time. The blue mushroom cap acts much like a glide panel, so look for it on your way through the cavern.

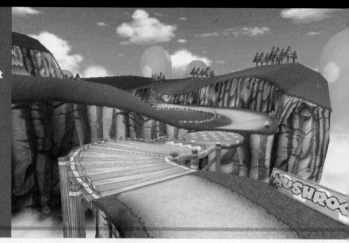

ROAD HAZARDS

GRASS: Stay off the grass to stay in the lead—unless you have a Mushroom! If you can't boost across the grass, keep your kart on the road.

STEEP DROPS: Whether you're drifting through turns or bouncing along giant mushrooms, take care to avoid nasty falls.

GOOMBAS: Dodge around these lumbering Goombas. A collision will cause your kart to spin out.

After landing from the bouncing mushroom, drift to the left and hold it around the bend. As you come around the corner, you'll see a fork in the road. Release your drift for a Mini-Turbo and take the path to the right. Bounce across the mushrooms and begin a drift to the left, holding it all the way around the next bend in the road.

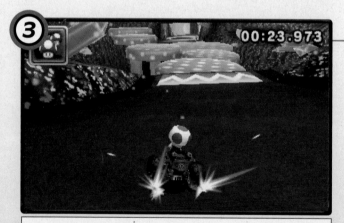

You enter a cavern that has quite a few bouncing mushrooms and crystals hanging from the walls. Release your drift for a boost and take the path of mushrooms that leads to the left. Remember to hop as you bounce on each mushroom for an extra boost of speed.

As you bounce off the blue mushroom, your glider will pop out. Fly through the large batch of coins as you glide down to the race path.

Time Trial

THE KART OF CHAMPIONS

 Character: Toad

 Kart: Pipe Frame

 Tires: Monster

Glider: Super Glider

1   00:04.942

Keep straight after you rocket start from the starting line. As you approach the first left turn, drift to the left for a Mini-Turbo. As soon as you receive the Mini-Turbo, drift to the right and hold it until you reach the dash panel. If you do this correctly, you receive a Mini-Turbo just before the dash panel. Make sure to straighten out as you bounce across the mushroom.

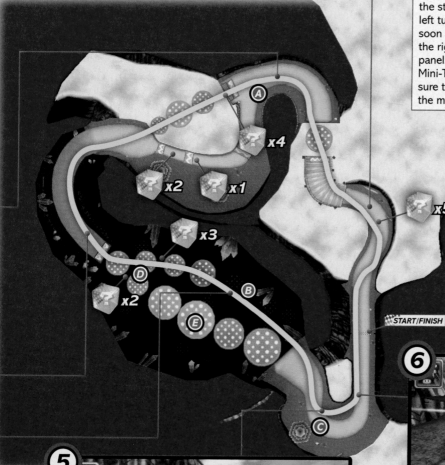

6   00:36.377

As you exit the grass area, release your drift for a Mini-Turbo toward the finish line. Straighten your kart as you cross the finish line for lap 1.

5   00:35.342

After landing from the glide, keep aiming straight for the grass ahead of you. Start a drift to the left and use one of your Mushrooms to speed through the grass. Avoid the Goombas that are in the area here.

INTRODUCTION

NEW CUPS

CLASSIC CUPS

BATTLE MAPS

Tactics for Laps 2 and 3

Use the same basic tactics to complete the remaining laps, but adjust your racing line to grab any coins you might need.

Grand Prix

When reaching the fork in the track, you can take the safer left path. This path has no bouncing mushrooms, unlike the right path. This is a safer option if there is a tight pack of racers on the right path.

When going through the cave with the crystals, take care when using the left path with the blue mushroom. If there is another racer behind you, they may hit you with a Shell, causing you to fall into the pit below.

You should always try to collect coins during the race, but the turn before the finish line is one of the easier spots to grab a quick four coins. Make sure to drift around this turn and collect the coins—just watch out for the Goombas in the area!

When bouncing off the mushrooms on this track, make sure you're traveling in the direction you want to go. Your momentum will carry you in the direction you were already going when you bounce!

Placing Bananas on the mushrooms is a great strategy. Oftentimes your opponents will be bouncing onto the next mushroom and won't be able to change the direction they are going, making them land right on the Banana you dropped!

Mirror Mode

After you master the standard track, test your skills in Mirror mode! The turns are reversed, but all of your tactics still apply.

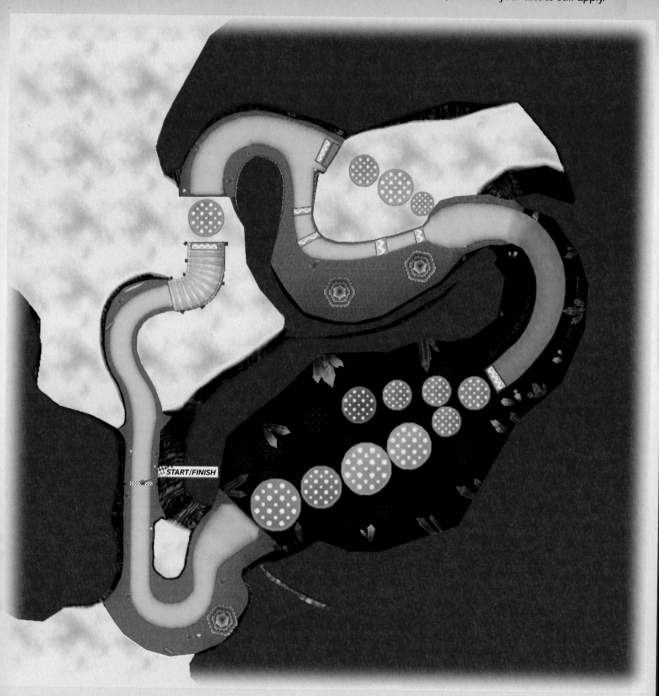

START/FINISH

DS Luigi's Mansion

Shell Cup

The sooner you get through this creepy course, the better! The mansion contains some tight turns, so watch those corners during each drift. The waterlogged grounds make the outdoor sections just as challenging. Use big drifts to maintain your speed through the mud, but take care not to crash into the roaming trees. Remember to look for the glide panel—why slog through the mud when you can take to the air?

ROAD HAZARDS

 GRASS: Keep your kart off the grass! This surface slows you down.

 MUD: Never drive straight into the mud! Drift over this surface to maintain your speed.

 CHANDELIERS: Every so often, elaborate light fixtures come crashing down. Try to avoid driving directly under them.

 WALKING TREES: Watch out for these mobile trees; they like creeping into the paths of reckless racers.

5

Upon exiting the mansion, you'll need to drift to the left, giving yourself enough time for a Mini-Turbo. Try to stay as close to the track's left side as you can when drifting.

6

When you complete your drift from the previous turn, use one of your Mushrooms to boost straight ahead through the grass. You'll see a ramp with a glide panel on it; make sure not to overshoot the ramp when you boost!

7

After you begin gliding, aim for the five coins floating in the air. This will keep you on the right path for landing back on the track.

8

After landing from gliding, drift to the left. Keep holding this drift while avoiding the walking trees.

Time Trial

THE KART OF CHAMPIONS

 Character: Luigi

 Kart: Egg 1

 Tires: Monster

Glider: Super Glider

3   00:13.558

When you come to the first turn in the mansion, start a drift to the right. Hold this drift through three corners, staying as close to the right wall as possible.

4   00:15.261

When you reach the bottom of the mansion, you'll see a line of coins. Release your drift for a boost, and collect two coins while taking the path to the right for another two coins.

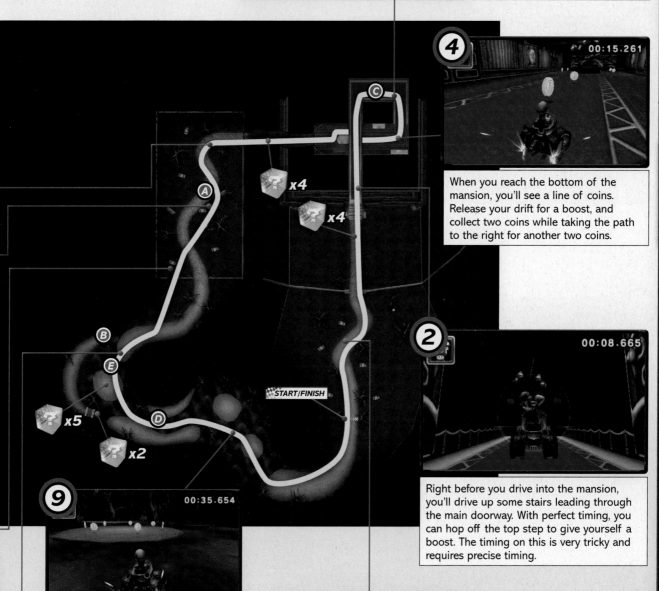

x4

x4

x5

x2

START/FINISH

2   00:08.665

Right before you drive into the mansion, you'll drive up some stairs leading through the main doorway. With perfect timing, you can hop off the top step to give yourself a boost. The timing on this is very tricky and requires precise timing.

9   00:35.654

After you pass the point where the track curves to the left, start a drift to the right. Hold this until you pass over the little piece of track that has seven rotating coins on it. Release your drift after collecting a few of the coins and begin a drift to the left, holding it until you see the finish line. Once you see the finish line, release your drift for a Mini-Turbo.

1   00:03.594

Begin with a rocket start from the starting line. When you reach the first turn, drift to the right until you see the road bend to the left. After drifting to the right for just a second, you'll need to drift immediately to the left, giving yourself the ability to do a Mini-Turbo.

INTRODUCTION

NEW CUPS

CLASSIC CUPS

BATTLE MAPS

Grand Prix

If you have a Mushroom when you reach the ramp with a glide panel, be sure to use it! It's a great shortcut and will help you soar above your opponents, keeping you mostly out of harm's way.

When you enter the muddy section of the track, you can find another path to the right that takes you up above the mud. This path has four easy-to-grab coins and a glide panel at the end with two item boxes.

The three turns going through the mansion is a great place to lay down a Banana. Opponents will have to work very hard to avoid them if you place them along the path they usually drift!

The walking trees in the mud area can be a very dangerous hazard since they can constantly change position on the track. You won't spin out if you run into one, but it will be just like hitting the stationary trees on the track.

When driving through the mud area of the track, you'll see a small section with five item boxes on it. If you can, try to grab more than one. You won't get any extra items out of it, but if you can stop your opponents behind you from getting an item, you'll be that much safer!

Mirror Mode

The setting is just as spooky, and all of the same tactics apply. Reverse the direction of every turn to match this Mirror mode track!

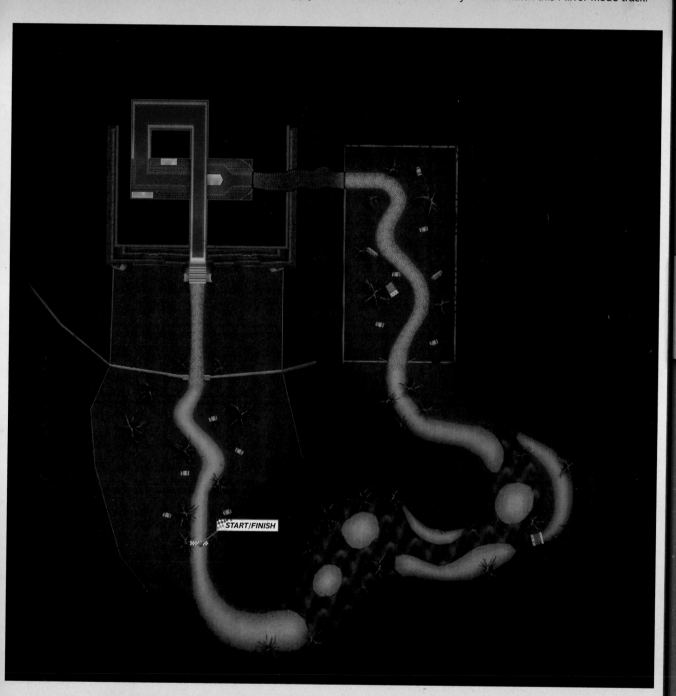

START/FINISH

N64 Koopa Beach

Banana Cup

Speed across the sands of this tropical course! Drift around the large rocks to maintain your speed, and make good use of the dash panels scattered throughout the area. There's a great shortcut near the end of each lap, but you'll need speed boost to reach it; make the most of your Mushrooms!

ROAD HAZARDS

 WATER: Your kart can handle water, but it performs better on dry land. You can tempt the tides along the coastline—just don't stray too far from the beach!

 TREES: Avoid the trees along the course. Be particularly careful when drifting near the rock walls.

 SIDESTEPPERS: Avoid the Sidesteppers along the course. Hitting one will cause you to spin out.

Hold your drift through the entire bend in the track. As you turn the corner, you will see a dash panel ahead of you. When you get closer to the ramp, release your drift for a speed boost toward the dash panel. Angle yourself so that after you take the dash panel, you don't land in the water.

Take the path that goes underneath the rock archway after landing from the dash panel jump. As you go forward, you'll see a small sand ramp and a ramp with a glide panel over the water. Use one of your Mushrooms to jump off the sand ramp and land on the ramp with the glide panel. As you glide through the air, be sure to land in the small cave straight ahead of you.

As you reach the end of the cave, begin a drift to the left immediately before you fall off the edge. Keep holding the drift as you land and make your way toward the dash panel ahead.

Time Trial

THE KART OF CHAMPIONS

Character: Koopa Troopa

Kart: Soda Jet

Tires: Sponge

Glider: Paraglider

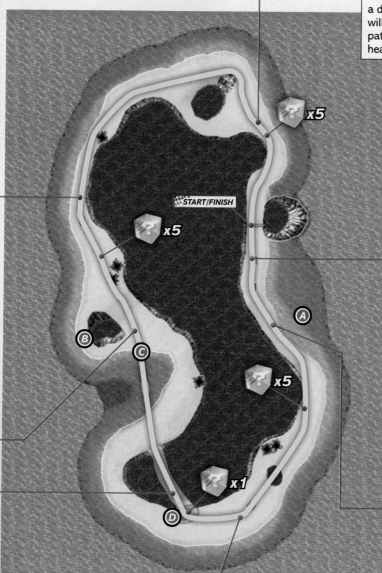

1 At the first turn from the starting line, start a drift to the left. As you hold the drift, you will come to a fork in the road. Take the path to the right, just under the rock turtle head.

7 Hit each of the dash panels that are located right before the finish line. Hop just as you leave each dash panel to get an extra boost of speed.

6 After landing from your glide, do an immediate drift to the left. Hold this just long enough to get a Mini-Turbo. Right after you release the boost, drift to the right. Hold this drift as you move toward the dash panels ahead of you.

5 Hold your drift until you line yourself up with the dash panel. As you glide through the air, fly over the turtle shell rock. Use the coin directly over the rock to guide your path, and grab it as you go by!

Tactics for Laps 2 and 3

Use the same basic tactics to complete the remaining laps. Adjust your racing line to collect needed coins, but try not to stray too far from the established route.

Grand Prix

Shortly before the finish is a line of coins. The water rises and falls in this area at regular intervals. If the water is down here when you pass by, be sure to take this path for an easy five coins!

If you are short on coins, take the path to the right for an easy three coins. This path may take a little longer than the one to the left, but the three coins can be worth it if you are in the lead.

Dropping a Banana just before the sand ramp can keep your opponents from using it for the shortcut. Just be careful when you do this, because you don't want to end up hitting your own Banana on the next lap!

When going around this corner, you see an item box just under the waterfall. Grab this even if you have an item already; at the very least, you'll stop an opponent behind you from getting it!

Mirror Mode

This mirrored track has all of the same great jumps and shortcuts! Just relearn the described tactics to compensate for the flipped turns.

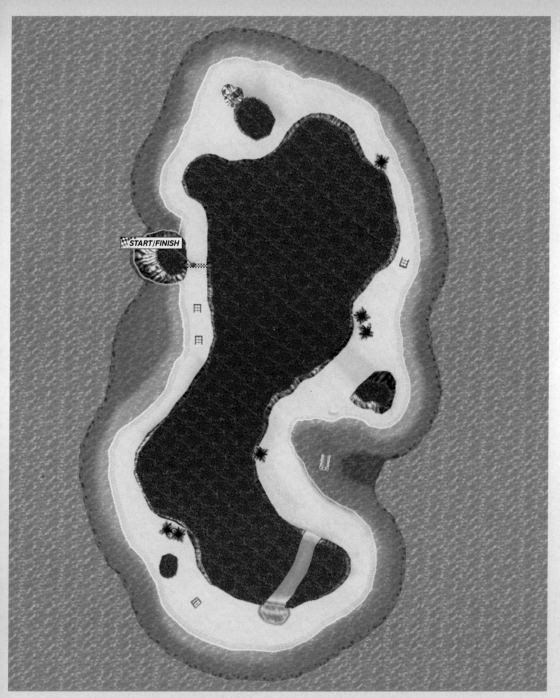

SNES Mario Circuit 2

Banana Cup

Find a path around the pipes and oil slicks as you race along this high-speed track. The sharp turns will test your drifting ability, but they also provide some convenient shortcuts. If you have a suitable item, you can cut a few corners on your way to the finish line!

ROAD HAZARDS

DIRT: Your kart will struggle with this loosely packed dirt. If you can't boost across it, it's best to stay on the road.

PIPES: Avoid the pipes placed throughout the course. Crashing into one of these obstacles will stop you in your tracks.

OIL SLICKS: Avoid the oil slicks at all costs! Driving over one of them will cause your kart to spin out.

After landing your jump from the ramp, immediately drift to the left and collect the three coins along the track. Release your drift for a Mini-Turbo boost and begin drifting to the right. Collect the three coins along the second turn as well.

As you approach the glide panel, try to line yourself up so you drive over the left portion of it. Hop as you go over the glide panel for an extra speed boost.

Begin a drift to the right as you approach this corner. Keep holding the drift and position your kart between the two pipes and the yellow portion of the track edge. Release your drift just before you hit the dirt to gain enough speed to make it through. You'll slow down slightly, but it is still faster than drifting around the entire bend in the road.

Time Trial

THE KART OF CHAMPIONS

 Character: Mario

 Kart: B Dasher

 Tires: Slick

 Glider: Super Glider

② 00:07.604

Hold your drift from the previous turn until you see a ramp off the main track. Release your drift for a Mini-Turbo boost as soon as you are lined up with the ramp. As you enter the dirt, use one of your Mushrooms for a speed boost to get you over the ramp.

① 00:03.573

Immediately after doing a rocket start from the start line, drift to the left. When the track turns to the right, immediately drift through the two pipes. Do a Mini-Turbo boost as you release your drift and begin drifting to the left around the next bend.

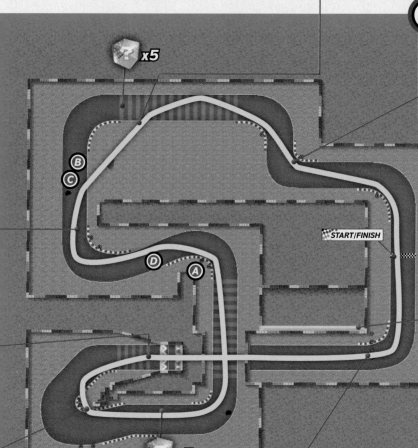

TIP

After driving across the glide panel, fly on to the yellow strip just to the left of the main road. This will give you a straight shot toward the finish line!

⑥ 00:56.048

Once you land from gliding, start a drift to the left to pass through the pipes on the road. Release the drift for a Mini-Turbo boost after you finish the turn and head toward the finish line. If you are short on coins, you can widen your drift for an additional three coins here.

Tactics for Laps 2 and 3

Use the same tactics to complete the remaining laps. After you collect 10 coins, consider adjusting your racing line; you can save a little time by taking each corner a bit tighter.

Grand Prix

If you manage to get a Star from an item box, go ahead and cut corners and drive right through pipes. You will knock them out of your way along with any of your opponents!

Dropping a Banana between the oil slick and the side of the road is a great tactic for slowing down your opponents. They'll need to carefully maneuver between both obstacles in order to not spin out!

Be careful following you opponents too closely; you may find yourself driving right into a Banana or Shell! Try to stay slightly to the left or right of other drivers to avoid this.

Red Shells can be extremely deadly on this track! If you are in the lead, make sure to always hold on to an item that can deflect a Red Shell, and keep an eye on that bottom screen to know what items your opponents hold.

Mirror Mode

Jump, drift, and boost your way through this flipped course. Use the same tactics, but take each turn in the opposite directions.

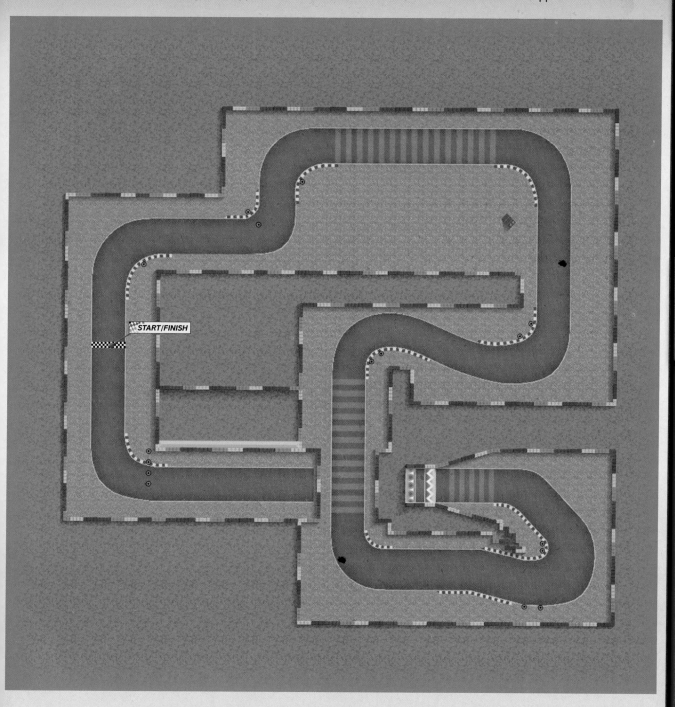

START/FINISH

Wii Coconut Mall

Banana Cup

If you keep an eye out for small inclines, you can turn many of the mall's obstacles to your advantage. Jump boost off of fountains and decorative trim to speed through this shopper's paradise. Cut through open shops, drift up looping walkways, then hit a glide panel to take the race to the parking lot!

ROAD HAZARDS

DECORATIVE FIXTURES: The mall is filled with decorative fixtures such as trees, columns, and planters. These objects might improve the setting, but they do tend to clutter the raceway. Take care to avoid hitting them.

ESCALATORS: Before you drive up an escalator, make sure they will carry you in the right direction. Avoid driving onto escalators that display red arrows.

ARCHES: As you glide out of the mall, avoid the arches in the parking lot.

CARS: The cars outside the mall are moving across the path. Avoid them!

③

00:10.983

As you exit the store, keep heading straight. Take the ramp off of the silver railing ahead of you. Make sure to hop to gain an extra speed boost here. Keep driving toward the escalators and take the one that has the arrows pointing in the direction you are going.

②

00:07.840

After exiting the escalator, steer to the right and stay on the current floor. As you drive to the right, you'll see a sign for a store called Delfino Dream. Begin a drift to the right and drive through the store for a great shortcut.

①

00:02.375

Upon starting, you'll see some stairs ahead of you. Veer slightly to the right and drive up the stairs leading to the right escalator. As you reach the top, time a hop perfectly and you'll gain a speed boost. At this point in the track, remember that the escalators can change directions at regular intervals; always be prepared to take the side where the arrows are pointing up.

⑨

00:43.410

With your speed boost from the previous dash panel, head toward the dash panel on the right-hand side now. Be very careful because there may be a car here directly in your path! It is possible to squeeze in between the wall and the car, as shown in the screenshot. After hitting the final dash panel, begin a drift to the right and head toward the finish line.

⑧

00:41.071

Once you finish gliding, try to land closer to the right-hand side of the road. Begin a drift to the right and begin sliding toward the dash panel on the road's left side. There are cars here that will be driving back and forth—avoid them at all costs! If you hit one, you'll topple over and lose precious seconds. After you hit the first dash panel, immediately steer to the right and you should avoid the first car.

TIP

You can use your Mushrooms on this track to quickly go over escalators that are moving in the wrong direction.

Time Trial

THE KART OF CHAMPIONS

 Character: Honey Queen

 Kart: Koopa Clown

Tires: Sponge

Glider: Paraglider

⑥ 00:27.116

Upon landing from your last jump over the fountain, begin a drift to the left around the next big bend. Collect the three coins around the turn. As you reach the top, stay to the left and head for a dash panel.

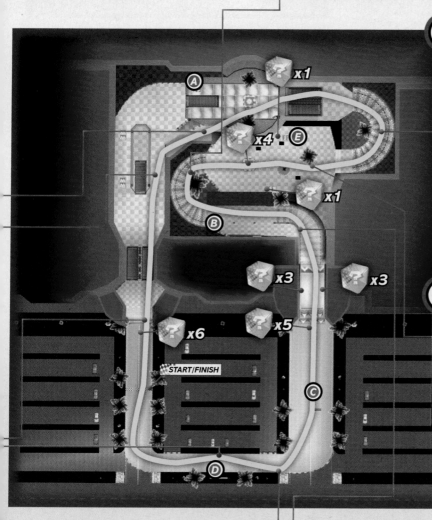

x1

Ⓐ

x4 Ⓔ

x1

Ⓑ

x3 x3

x6 x5

START/FINISH

Ⓒ

Ⓓ

④ 00:19.044

Drift to the right around the big bend ahead, and try to collect at least two of the coins as you build up a Mini-Turbo boost.

⑤ 00:22.068

As you drive through this next section, try to keep your kart lined up with the palm trees. You'll want to hop off of each small section surrounding each palm tree to gain Mini-Turbo boosts. Keep driving toward the fountain past the palm trees and hop over it as well for another Mini-Turbo boost.

⑦ HAVE A NICE DAY! 00:32.675

Once you gain the speed boost from the dash panel, begin a drift to the right. After turning slightly, you'll see the exit to the mall. Keep driving forward and hit the glide panel to begin gliding over the outdoor area. Make sure you hop as you hit the glide panel for an extra boost!

Tactics for Laps 2 and 3

Use the same basic tactics to complete the remaining laps, but make a few small adjustments to your racing line. The cars in the parking lot will might be in different locations, and the escalators switch direction each time you complete a lap.

Grand Prix

If you take the lower level of the track in the mall, hit every dash panel to keep up with racers who take the top level.

When you reach this portion of the track, you can take the path to the right to reach an area with six item boxes on either side of a palm tree. This route may be the better option if your opponents all take the upper path.

After landing from your glide, you'll see a metal ramp ahead of you. If you can correctly time a hop off of it, you'll gain a Mini-Turbo boost that can help speed you up if you are falling behind your opponents.

Be careful in the section with the cars moving back and forth. This is a very dangerous section that can easily turn disastrous. If you have a Banana, this is a great section to drop it in, making it even more difficult for your opponents to make it through safely!

If you are forced to the left or right side of this room, drive over the dash panel and pick up the item box. If you are falling behind in the race, it could contain an item necessary to get you back in the lead!

Mirror Mode

This flipped track has all of the same options as the original; it just presents them a little differently. As long as you take each turn in the opposite direction, these tactics are just as effective.

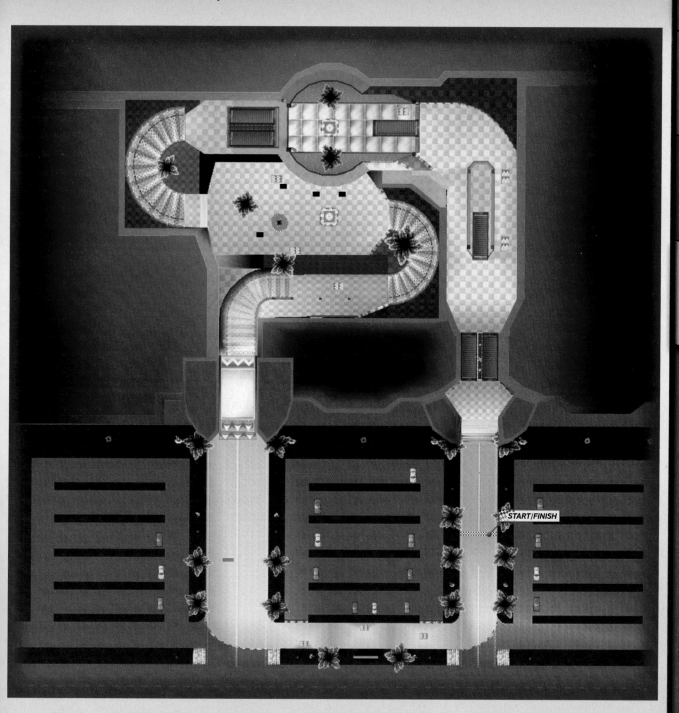

START/FINISH

DS Waluigi Pinball

Banana Cup

The track takes you through a giant pinball machine, but you aren't here to play around. Dodge pinballs, bumpers, and flippers as you wind your way through this crazy course. Drift through each turn, hop into every jump, and dodge the extra balls that appear throughout the event.

ROAD HAZARDS

 PINBALLS: These giant pinballs will topple your kart if you let them. Keep your distance!

 BUMPERS: When you touch a bumper, it knocks you away. Some bumpers are mobile, so keep your eyes open.

 FLIPPERS: Don't get hit by one of these giant flippers. When a flipper lights up, give it a wide berth.

TIP
Try holding down on the Circle Pad as you are gliding on this track to gain even more speed! This move only works on tracks where you can glide, but not move left or right.

The dash panel ahead has five coins floating in front of it. Attempt to grab a coin each lap if you don't have the maximum ten.

If you are fast enough on your time, you can get ahead of the giant pinball that rolls down the track. If you end up behind it, take care not to run into it or you will topple over!

Upon reaching this turn, start a drift to the right and continue holding it until you reach the next straight portion of the track. You'll want to stay close to the inner section of the track, but feel free to grab the five coins lined up on the center portion.

Take care when navigating this section of the track; there are bumpers that can knock you around, pinballs that can topple you, and flippers that can push you back. When reaching the end of this portion of track, drive over the arrows labeled on the ground to avoid being hit by the flippers.

Time Trial

THE KART OF CHAMPIONS

W **Character:** Wario

Kart: Bruiser

Tires: Slim

Glider: Beast Glider

1 After landing from your glide, immediately drift to the left and stay as close as possible to the wall. Keep holding this until you see a small ramp with four arrows on it. Release the drift for a Mini-Turbo boost and hop over the ramp for an extra speed boost.

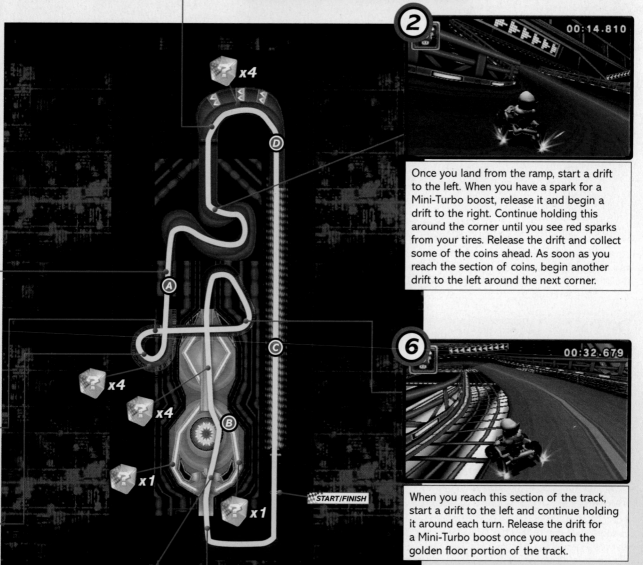

2 Once you land from the ramp, start a drift to the left. When you have a spark for a Mini-Turbo boost, release it and begin a drift to the right. Continue holding this around the corner until you see red sparks from your tires. Release the drift and collect some of the coins ahead. As soon as you reach the section of coins, begin another drift to the left around the next corner.

6 When you reach this section of the track, start a drift to the left and continue holding it around each turn. Release the drift for a Mini-Turbo boost once you reach the golden floor portion of the track.

8 Begin a drift to the left when you drive onto the purple floor. Have your drift travel through the two coins ahead of you, and continue to hold the drift and drive through the next two coins as well. This brings you to the finish line.

TIP

Use your Mushrooms to recover from obstacles hitting you, such as pinballs!

Tactics for Laps 2 and 3

Use the same tactics to complete the remaining laps, but watch out for rolling pinballs! Adjust your racing line as needed.

When being launched through the long tunnel, use a Red Shell on an opponent if you have one. They'll be hit and fall just outside the end of the tunnel, allowing you to pull ahead!

Grand Prix

Take care when in the lead on this section of the course; you may end up directly behind the pinball! If you hit the dash panel with the pinball in front of you, it will end badly.

Once you land from the long tunnel, you can use the dash panels located along the track's outer edge, but you'll possibly miss collecting one of the item boxes along the inner portion.

When driving through this portion of the track, a somewhat safer option is staying on the far left or far right side. You won't have to worry about bumpers, but still keep an eye out for pinballs. There is also a single item box on either side, which can be enough to turn the tide of a race!

Mirror Mode

Use the same tactics to speed through this flipped track—just remember to take each turn in the opposite direction.

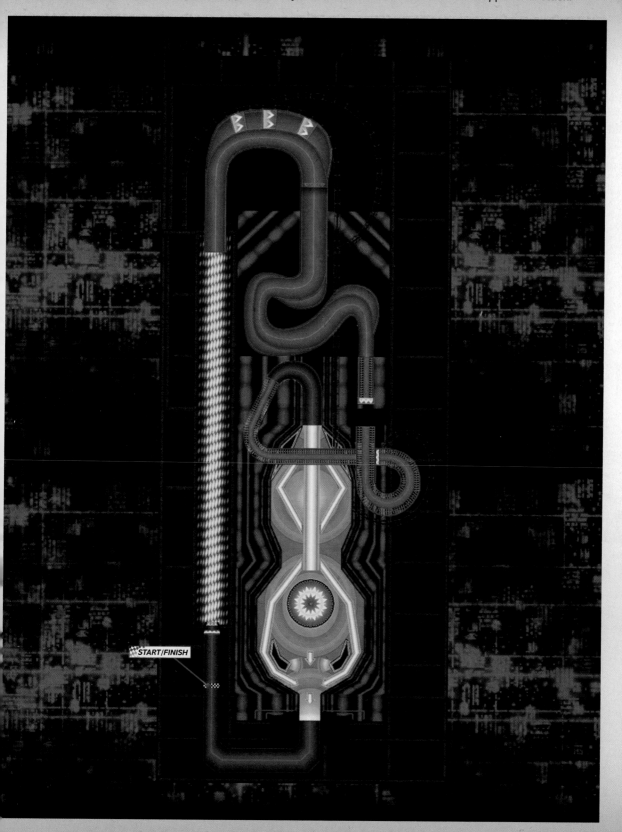

START/FINISH

N64 Kalimari Desert

Leaf Cup

This desert course follows a simple path, but the train circling the area makes things a little more complicated. Use caution each time you approach the railroad tracks; a big crash can knock you right out of the lead. There are some nice shortcuts along the course, but don't venture off-road unless you have a Mushroom handy!

ROAD HAZARDS

 DARK SAND: Unless you have a Mushroom, keep your kart out of the dark sand. Your kart struggles on this low-traction surface.

 CACTI: If you venture off-road, remember to avoid the cacti. Crashing into one of these will turn a shortcut into a disaster.

 TRAIN: Watch out for the train circling the area. Don't get blindsided by this powerful locomotive!

Begin a drift to the right around the next bend in the track and only hold it until you see blue sparks from your tires. As soon as the sparks appear, release the drift for a Mini-Turbo boost. You'll need this boost to ensure you cross the tracks before the train arrives; you don't want to have to stop and wait for it!

After crossing the tracks, begin a drift to the left. Release this drift and cross over the small platform, hop as you leave the platform for a Mini-Turbo boost. Be sure to collect the coin as you jump off of the ramp.

Time Trial

THE KART OF CHAMPIONS

Character: Shy Guy

Kart: Bolt Buggy

Tires: Red Monster

Glider: Beast Glider

2 00:05.764

Immediately after you perform the sharp turn into the dirt, use one of your Mushrooms for a speed boost toward the ramp ahead. Continue up the ramp and hop as you pass over the glide panel. Soar over the train tracks and land just before the four coins on the track.

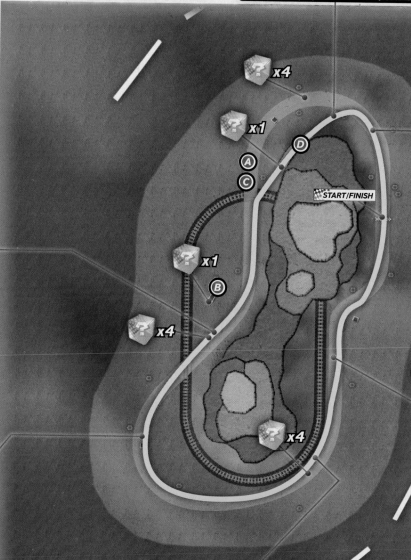

1 00:02.956

Rocket start off the starting line and begin a drift to the left, collecting at least two of the coins ahead of you. Continue holding the drift until just before you pass a cactus after the coins. Release the drift and turn sharply to the left.

6 00:32.360

Upon landing, line yourself up with the two gold coins immediately in front of you. As soon as you collect them, begin a drift to the right, followed shortly by a drift to the left. Drift through the three coins ahead of you and cross the finish line to complete the first lap.

5 00:29.120

As soon as you are lined up with the next ramp in the road, release your drift for a Mini-Turbo boost. Continue heading toward the ramp and hop as you go over the ramp for a Mini-Turbo boost.

INTRODUCTION · NEW CUPS · CLASSIC CUPS · BATTLE MAPS

Tactics for Laps 2 and 3

Use the same tactics to complete the remaining laps, but adjust your racing line if you need additional coins.

Grand Prix

Oftentimes your opponents will have to stop and wait for the train to pass. This is the perfect time to hit them with a Shell and speed on by! Be careful if you ever have to stop for the train; your opponents may do the same thing to you!

If you have a Mushroom when you reach this section of the track, feel free to use it and cross the dirt toward this ramp. At the ramp's top is a glide panel and a single item box. Using this path can also help you fly over the tracks if a train is present!

Right before either of the train tracks is a great place to lay down a Banana. This can throw off your opponents and maybe even cause them to slide directly into one of the trains!

If you have a Mushroom, take the path to the left here. You'll need to make a sharp turn, but the ramp's top has a glide panel and an item box. The glide panel can be especially helpful if there is a train on the tracks—you can fly right over it!

Mirror Mode

Use the same great shortcuts when you race on this mirrored course, but remember that each turn is flipped.

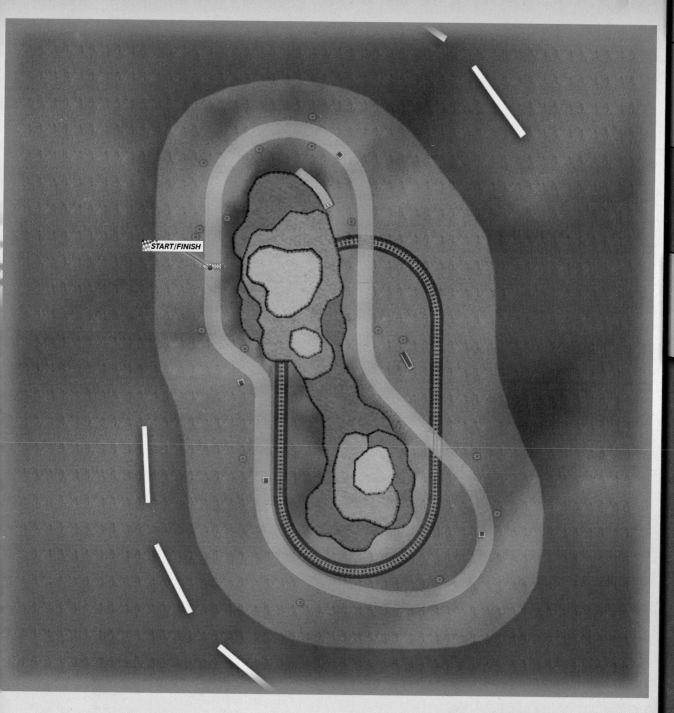

START/FINISH

DS DK Pass

Leaf Cup

You'll face some rough conditions on this winding course. The gentle snowfall limits visibility, so keep your eyes on the road. Dodge grinning snowmen and runaway snowballs as you drift, jump, and boost your way through DK Pass!

ROAD HAZARDS

 SNOW: Avoid driving across snow; without a boost, your kart will struggle on this low-traction surface.

STEEP DROPS: A tumble down the mountain will cost you valuable time. Watch those turns!

 SNOWMEN: Crashing through these cheery snowmen will send you into a spin. Steer around them to keep your speed up.

 SNOWBALLS: Stay clear of these giant snowballs. They tend to blend in with the environment, so stay alert.

5
`00:29.886`

Drive toward the ramp with the two coins floating in front of it. Make sure you hop as you leave the ramp for a Mini-Turbo boost, and grab one of the coins as you jump! Drift to the left as you land and proceed around the corner. Hop as you pass over the next ramp and begin a drift to the right once on the ground again.

6
`00:36.892`

Release the drift you were holding before for a boost, and line yourself up with the ramp ahead. Hop as you go over the ramp for a Mini-Turbo boost. Take care when landing your jump from the ramp; a giant snowball is ahead of you.

8
`00:46.824`

Once you land, begin a drift to the right and proceed around the corner. Take extra care around this turn, as there will be some snowmen in the way. Drift carefully around them and then release the drift for a Mini-Turbo boost toward the finish line.

1
`00:02.556`

As soon as you leave the starting line, begin a drift to the right, and hold it while proceeding into the tunnel. Once you see the blue sparks form on your tires, release the drift for a Mini-Turbo boost. Collect some of the coins as you drive through the tunnel.

Time Trial

THE KART OF CHAMPIONS

DK Character: Donkey Kong

Kart: Bolt Buggy

Tires: Red Monster

Glider: Paraglider

④ 00:24.552

Shortly after passing the snowball rolling down the road, start a drift to the left. As you go around the corner, pick up the four coins.

③ 00:21.224

Start a drift going around this big curve, and hold it until you see red sparks coming off your tires for a Mini-Turbo boost. Release the drift and drive up to the next turn to begin a drift to the right. Try to drift toward the red fence past the snowman, but be careful not to hit the fence or you'll lose all your momentum! The reason for this is to dodge the giant snowball that is rolling down the road.

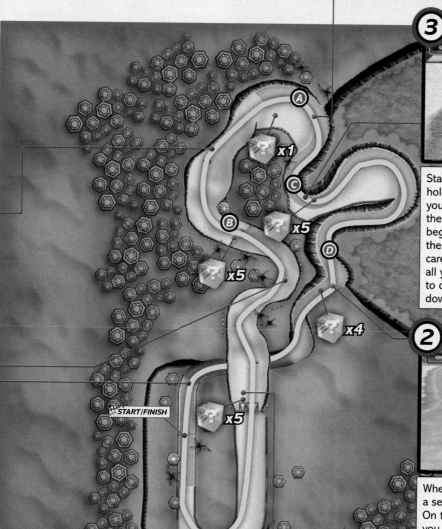

START/FINISH

A

x1

C

B

x5

x5

D

x4

x5

② 00:09.765

When you exit the tunnel, drift left for just a second, quickly followed by a drift right. On the third curve, drift left and hold it until you are able to perform a Mini-Turbo boost. Immediately after receiving the boost, begin a drift to the right and carefully pass by the snowman on the road.

⑦ 00:41.327

If the snowball isn't in your way, go ahead and hop off the next ramp down the track. Keep driving forward and hop as you pass over the glide panel for an extra boost in speed. As you glide through the air, you'll see two clumps of coins. Glide through the right clump and grab as many of the coins as you can.

Tactics for Laps 2 and 3

Use the same basic tactics to complete the remaining laps. Adjust your racing line if you need to collect a few extra coins, but make the most of every drift!

Grand Prix

Dropping a Banana at the end of the coins here is a great move for slowing down your opponents or stopping them from collecting the coins! If they drift through the coins, they'll probably run into a Banana!

When reaching this section of the track, grab one of the item boxes on the left side. You can get an item and jump off the small ram for a Mini-Turbo boost!

If you have a Mushroom, you can use it to take a shortcut over the snowy hill ahead, allowing you to get ahead of the competition!

Be very careful around the curves in this section of the track; one mistake and you can go over the edge. Also watch for opponents near the edge here. If you are using a heavier character, you can bump them off the cliff!

Mirror Mode

The turns are just as crazy, but they each head in the opposite direction when you race along this flipped track!

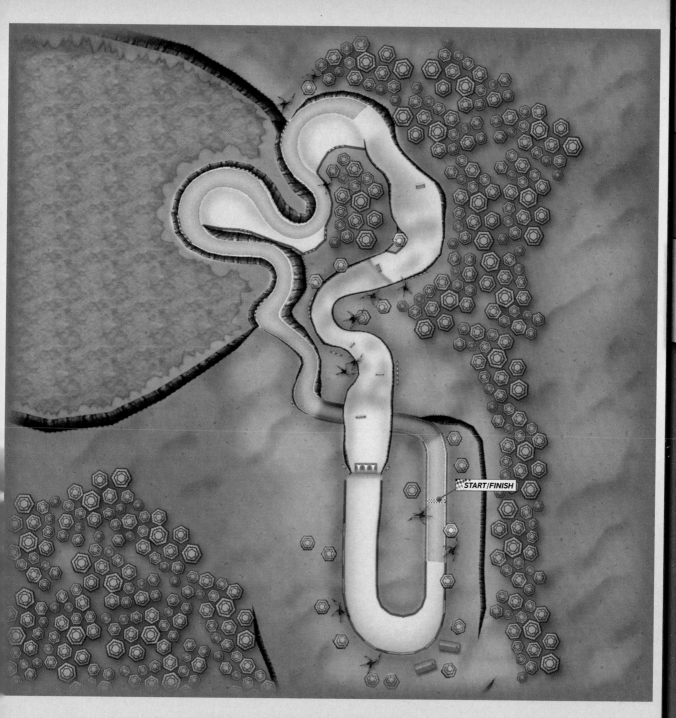

START/FINISH

GC Daisy Cruiser

Leaf Cup

This luxury liner has a few alternate paths, so choose your course wisely. Race across the deck, through the dining room, and—if it suits you—into the ship's aquarium! Most of your boosts will come from big drifts, but there are a few dash panels to help speed you through the course.

ROAD HAZARDS

 COLUMNS: Watch out for these columns as you speed through the dining room!

 TABLES: Once they start sliding, these tables move quickly. Slip past them to stay on course.

 CLAMPY: The ship's aquarium has a variety of aquatic life, but Clampys are your biggest concern. Don't get caught in their snapping jaws!

With your Mini-Turbo boost, drive through the pool and down the ramp ahead. There will be arrows pointing exactly where you need to go. As you come out of the pool, start a drift to the left. Hold this drift all the way down the ramp, and then release it as you hit the straightaway.

After you rocket start, take the path to the starting line's left. As soon as you drive onto the silver track, begin a drift to the right. Hold the drift just until you get blue sparks for a Mini-Turbo boost.

Right when you land from your jump, begin a drift to the right, holding it all the way around the turn in the track. When you see the ramp heading upward, release your drift and continue driving forward. When you reach the ramp's end, hop right when you go airborne to gain another Mini-Turbo boost as you head for the finish line.

As soon as you create blue sparks from your drift, release it to get a Mini-Turbo boost. Immediately begin a drift to the left and hold it as you drift into the small pool of water. This will drop you into the ship's underwater section.

Time Trial

THE KART OF CHAMPIONS

 Character: Daisy

 Kart: Tiny Tug

 Tires: Sponge

Glider: Peach Parasol

(3) 00:14.014

Line yourself up with the right row of coins down the straightaway, and collect them as you drive a straight line through them. As soon as you are lined up with the coins, use one of your Mushrooms to boost you into the next room.

(4) 00:17.701

Stay between the two racing lines as you enter this room, but slowly start moving toward the left racing line. Be careful as you drive through this room, as the table can slide right into you or block your path. Once you are near the end of this room, begin a drift to the right to enter the next hallway.

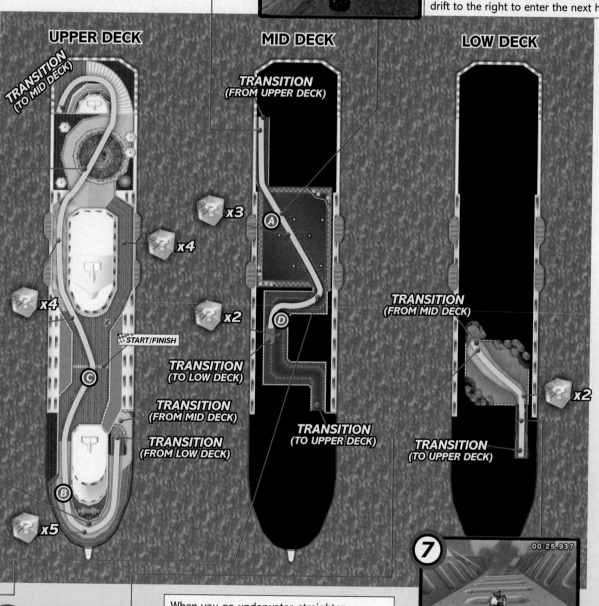

UPPER DECK

TRANSITION (TO MID DECK)

x3

x4

x4

START/FINISH

(C)

TRANSITION (TO LOW DECK)

TRANSITION (FROM MID DECK)

TRANSITION (FROM LOW DECK)

(B)

x5

MID DECK

TRANSITION (FROM UPPER DECK)

(A)

x2

(D)

TRANSITION (TO UPPER DECK)

LOW DECK

TRANSITION (FROM MID DECK)

x2

TRANSITION (TO UPPER DECK)

(7) 00:25.937

Drive across the two dash panels and receive a quick burst of speed, sending you flying out of the water. If you hop as soon as you leave the water, you can get an extra Mini-Turbo boost.

(6) 00:22.815

When you go underwater, straighten yourself out so you are on the main path. This is also the time to release your drift you were holding, giving you the extra boost you need to get out of the water more quickly. Drive between the two Clampys while staying on the path, heading toward the two dash panels.

Tactics for Laps 2 and 3

Use the same basic tactics to complete the remaining laps, but remember to steer around the sliding tables.

There is a path to the right that you can take from the starting line. It is almost exactly the same as the left path but makes it a bit harder to drift properly into the next area.

Grand Prix

As you drive through the section with the sliding tables, you'll notice some item boxes that slide around as well. Try to grab one of these if you can, but don't waste too much time chasing after them!

If you stay out of the water, you have access to two item boxes. This path may be a little less treacherous but doesn't offer the speed boosts that the underwater path does.

Placing Bananas in front of the ramp before the finish line is a great way to slow opponents down. Most likely they'll be coming off a drift and will struggle to avoid them!

144 primagames.com

Mirror Mode

The established tactics still work, but the turns have all flipped. Race through this luxury liner in Mirror mode!

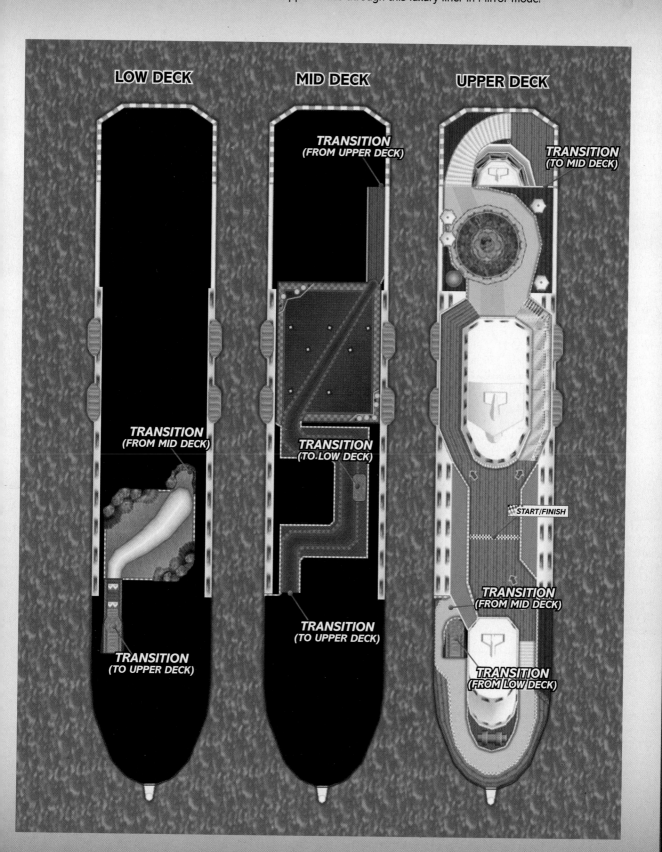

LOW DECK

MID DECK

UPPER DECK

TRANSITION
(FROM UPPER DECK)

TRANSITION
(TO MID DECK)

TRANSITION
(FROM MID DECK)

TRANSITION
(TO LOW DECK)

START/FINISH

TRANSITION
(TO UPPER DECK)

TRANSITION
(FROM MID DECK)

TRANSITION
(TO UPPER DECK)

TRANSITION
(FROM LOW DECK)

Wii Maple Treeway

Leaf Cup

There are a few spots where you can fall off this track, so watch your drift through the wilder turns. The twisting roots create a few alternate paths, and numerous dash panels help push you around the course. The Wigglers circling the treetop take up a lot of space. Find a path around them to avoid their stomping feet.

ROAD HAZARDS

 STEEP DROPS: Don't fall off the winding branches. Each slip will cost you valuable time!

 WIGGLERS: These massive Wigglers circle the treetop. Don't get caught underfoot!

3

`00:17.446`

As you approach the straightaway, release your drift for a nice Mini-Turbo boost toward the next turn.

6

`00:30.547`

After leaving the treetop, begin a drift to the right. Keep drifting until you are lined up with the dash panel located on the track's left side. Release the drift just before touching the dash panel, but make sure you are lined up with the second dash panel ahead. Weave from the first dash panel to the second one, making sure to drive over each one.

7

`00:36.012`

After receiving the boost from the second dash panel, begin a drift to the right. Hug the inner part of the track while collecting the coins along your path. Release your drift as soon as you see the portion of the track with three arrows on it. As you drive over the three arrows, hop just as you go airborne to gain an extra Mini-Turbo boost.

4

`00:20.802`

After the straightaway, you'll reach a path that winds up the tree. Perform a drift to the left and stay as close to the inside of the track as possible.

5

`00:24.444`

Navigate the treetop carefully, as there are two giant Wigglers walking around. If possible, drive through the piles of leaves to possibly pick up some more coins. Just avoid the Wigglers at all costs!

Time Trial

THE KART OF CHAMPIONS

Character: Wiggler

Kart: Egg 1

Tires: Sponge

Glider: Flower Glider

①

Shortly after leaving the starting line, begin drifting to the left to get a Mini-Turbo boost. When you receive the boost, start drifting to the right to gain another Mini-Turbo boost. Release the previous boost when you see sparks from your tires and begin another drift to the left. Use one of your Mushrooms as you go around the last corner, while still holding the drift. Release the drift as you approach the dash panels.

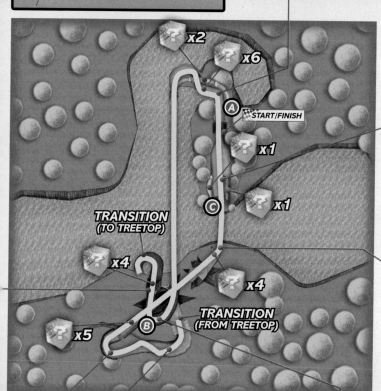

START/FINISH

TRANSITION
(TO TREETOP)

TRANSITION
(FROM TREETOP)

TRANSITION
(ONTO TREETOP)

TRANSITION
(OFF OF TREETOP)

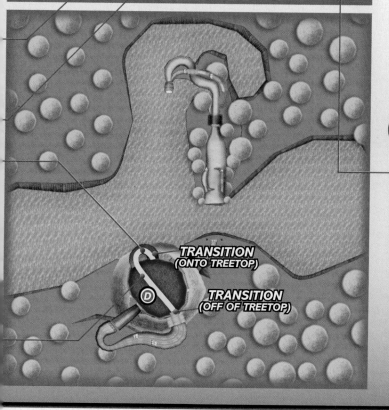

⑨ 00:52.302

As you land from your glide, keep driving straight. You'll see a coin directly on top of a tree root. Grab the coin, and hop when you pick it up to get a Mini-Turbo boost.

⑧ 00:47.611

Keep heading straight through the course, making sure to grab any coins you can. Begin a drift when the road starts to turn left. You should have just enough time to get a Mini-Turbo boost just before you hit the glide panel.

② 00:14.778

Once you land from the long glide, begin drifting to the right and directly through the pile of leaves. A coin will pop out along the path that you are drifting; collect it as you continue down the course.

Tactics for Laps 2 and 3

Use the same basic tactics to complete the remaining laps, but adjust your racing line to collect missed coins and avoid moving hazards. Perform big drifts to charge Mini-Turbos and Super Mini-Turbos, and use your remaining Mushrooms to cut over to the hidden path. Above all, make sure you stay out of that lake!

Grand Prix

Right when the race begins, you'll notice a path to the right. There is some terrain that will slow you down if you take this path, but it is a safe option at the start of a race. There are also two item boxes on this path, as well as some dash panels to help speed you along.

The piles of leaves along the track can contain coins, Mushrooms, and other helpful items. They can also contain items that slow you down, such as Bananas, so be cautious when you drive through the piles.

After gliding, you can land on either side of the main path. Each of these spots has a single item box and a dash panel.

Take extra care when navigating the treetop. You might come face-to-face with a Wiggler, and it isn't going to care if you are in its way; it will walk right over you! This area can be really good for putting down Bananas, causing your opponents to avoid the Wigglers and the obstacle you set for them.

Mirror Mode

This course has all of the big drifts and exciting jumps of the original, but each turn takes you in the opposite direction.

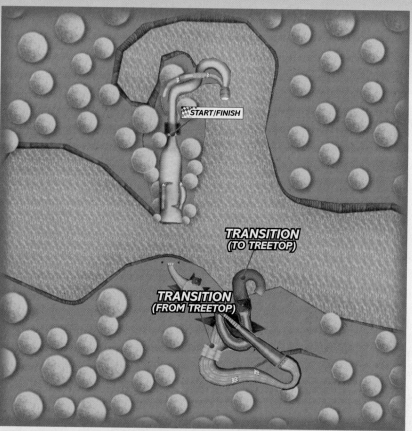

START/FINISH

TRANSITION
(TO TREETOP)

TRANSITION
(FROM TREETOP)

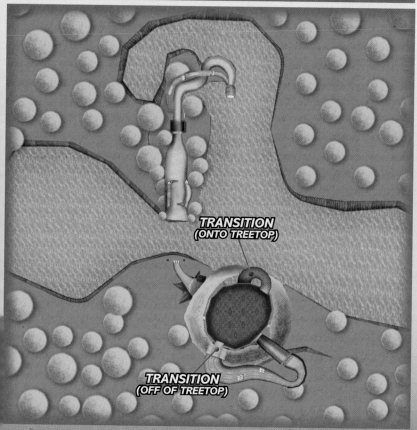

TRANSITION
(ONTO TREETOP)

TRANSITION
(OFF OF TREETOP)

Wii Koopa Cape

Lightning Cup

Drift, glide, and slide your way through this wild course! Dodge Goombas on the way to the water, then glide in the stream and go with the flow. You can cut a few corners along the way, but don't get caught in the waterfall at the end of each lap!

ROAD HAZARDS

 GRASS: Unless you have a Mushroom boost, stay off the grass!

STEEP DROPS: Whether you're knocked off the track or swept over the waterfall, slipping off the course can ruin your chances for victory.

GOOMBAS: Avoid the Goombas near the start of each lap.

 CHEEP CHEEPS: When you head into the water, expect to find Cheep Cheeps swimming against the current. They'll swim right past you if you move aside.

4 Continue gliding in a straight path. You want to land just before the big left turn ahead of you. When you land, stay in the water and drift to the left. Go under the rock archway and turn toward the grassy area next to the Red Shell.

1 As you leave the starting line, drive toward the left side of the dash panels ahead of you. As you land, begin a drift to the left. Line up your drift with the ramp ahead and release it for a Mini-Turbo boost. Remember to hop as you leave the ramp for an extra speed boost.

5 As you approach the grassy area, use one of your Mushrooms. This will boost you through the shortcut and keep you at top speed as you move through the grass.

8 As soon as you land again, begin a drift to the right. Collect one of the coins around the bend and release your drift for a Mini-Turbo boost as soon as the water on your right ends.

Time Trial

THE KART OF CHAMPIONS

 Character: Koopa Troopa

 Kart: Cact-X

 Tires: Standard

 Glider: Flower Glider

③ Begin a drift to the left around the next corner, and hold it until you are lined up with the glide panel ahead of you. Release it for a Mini-Turbo boost and hop as you go across the panels.

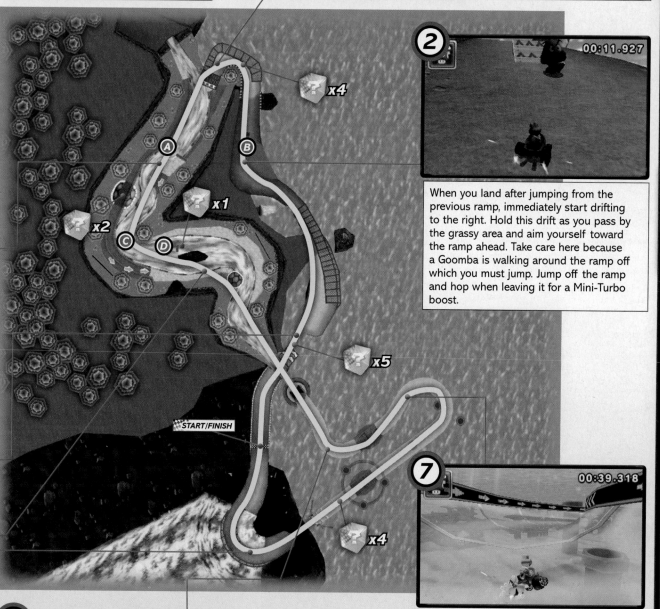

② When you land after jumping from the previous ramp, immediately start drifting to the right. Hold this drift as you pass by the grassy area and aim yourself toward the ramp ahead. Take care here because a Goomba is walking around the ramp off which you must jump. Jump off the ramp and hop when leaving it for a Mini-Turbo boost.

⑥ Keep heading forward and dive into the water. As you approach the turn, start drifting to the left. Take care here—there are Cheep Cheeps swimming that can stop you dead in your tracks if you run into them. When the track straightens out, release your drift for a Mini-Turbo boost.

⑦ At the next turn, start drifting to the right, all the way around the bend. When the track straightens, release your drift and try to line up with some of the coins; collect at least two of them. When you go under the green turtle shell, you'll see some arrows on the track. Hop just as you leave the arrows for a Mini-Turbo boost. Keep heading toward the dash panels and remember to hop just as you leave the water for yet another Mini-Turbo boost.

INTRODUCTION · NEW CUPS · CLASSIC CUPS · BATTLE MAPS

Tactics for Laps 2 and 3

Use the same basic tactics to complete the remaining laps. Adjust your racing to collect additional coins or to avoid roaming Goombas and Cheep Cheeps.

Grand Prix

While gliding through the air, take the path under the blue turtle shell if you need an item.

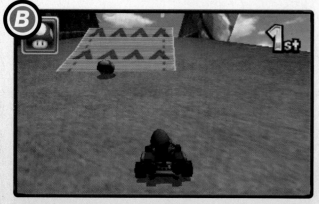

If you have a Fire Flower at this part of the track, you can shoot a Goomba to turn it into a Mushroom! Grab the Mushroom for an extra burst of speed and pass your opponents.

While traveling down the river, you may notice an occasional item box. Grab it and take advantage of the extra item!

If you haven't managed to get an item box yet on the river, there is one directly to the left of the rock archway, right in front of a ramp. If you can, grab the item box and hop at the same time to get a Mini-Turbo boost!

Mirror Mode

After you master these tactics, test your skill in Mirror mode. If you remember to take each turn in the opposite direction, you shouldn't have any trouble on this flipped track.

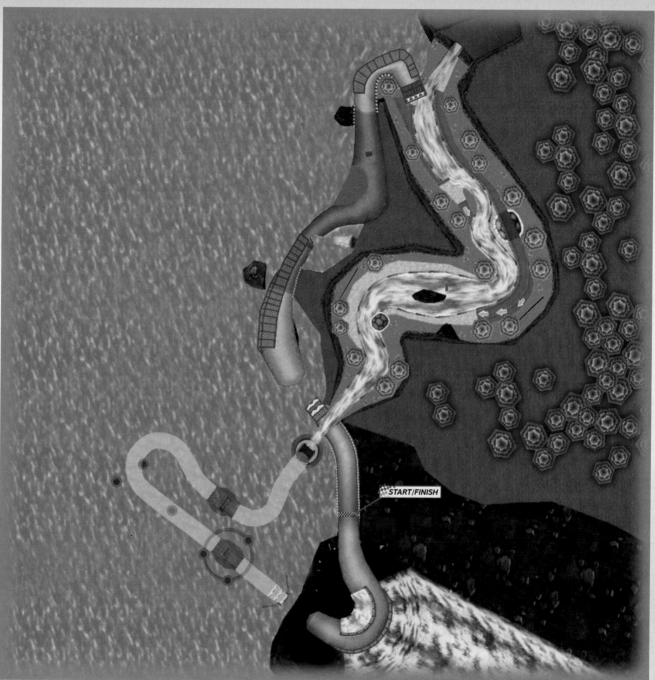

START/FINISH

MARIO KART 7

GC Dino Dino Jungle

Lightning Cup

This course has its share of hazards, but avoiding falls should be your main concern. There's a big shortcut toward the end of each lap; you'll save a lot of time if you use the glide panel. Use jump boosts and big drifts to speed through the course, and watch yourself around that huge dinosaur.

ROAD HAZARDS

 MUD: Never drive straight through mud without using a Mushroom. If you can't boost, use a drift to help maintain your speed.

 STEEP DROPS: Narrow bridges and massive pits make for some risky drifts. Stay in control to stay on the track!

  DINOSAUR: Watch for this dinosaur near the beginning and end of each lap. This beast is so large, it creates two different hazards!

 GEYSERS: Geysers erupt at regular intervals. Make sure you don't get caught in the blast!

⑦

When landing from your glide, start turning right so that you can hit the next glide panel. When gliding here, try to fly underneath the dinosaur's neck to save a little time.

⑥

Start drifting and collect any coins you are able to as you enter the enclosed area. When you enter the large open cavern, take a sharp turn to the right. Release the drift when you are lined up with the glide panel, then use one of your Mushrooms to speed across the mud. Remember to hop as you go across the glide panel for an extra speed boost.

⑤

As you approach the turn ahead, start drifting to the right. Hold this drift until you reach the top of the wooden platforms.

④

Take the lowest bridge just ahead of you as you come out of the cave. You'll need to turn to the right in order to see it. Keep moving forward and drive over the dash panels ahead of you.

Time Trial

THE KART OF CHAMPIONS

 Character: Yoshi

 Kart: Egg 1

 Tires: Monster

Glider: Swooper

① `00:04.180`

Begin the track with a rocket start and head straight to the first turn. As you approach the first turn, start drifting to the left, holding it all the way around the bend. Release the drift for a Mini-Turbo boost as soon as the track starts turning to the right.

② `00:06.005`

Drift slightly to the right to go across the log in front of you. Try to go over the exact spot where there is a coin. Hop as you go over the log for a Mini-Turbo boost.

x2 Ⓒ Ⓑ
x5
START/FINISH
Ⓓ
x2
x2
x2 Ⓐ x4

③ `00:13.210`

Keep driving straight and go just slightly to the right of the dinosaur's feet. When you enter the cave, immediately start drifting to the right. When you see sparks from your tires, release the drift and begin drifting to the left. Hold this drift for just a second and begin drifting to the right as you come out of the cave.

⑧ `00:41.149`

After passing the dinosaur, keep driving down the track until the next turn. Begin a drift to the left just after you drop down slightly from a wooden platform. Release the drift for a Mini-Turbo boost. Keep hopping as you drop down each level for an extra speed boost.

⑨ `00:42.645`

Be careful to avoid the geysers ahead. However, do drive over one of the small bumps in the ground; if you hop as you go over one, you get a Mini-Turbo boost.

Tactics for Laps 2 and 3

Use the same basic tactics to complete the remaining laps. Avoid the dinosaur's head and legs, and keep an eye on those geysers!

Grand Prix

There are three paths that you can take once you reach this section of the track. Each path has two item boxes, but only the lower path contains a dash panel.

As you enter the large open cavern, you have two paths that you can take. The path to the right has a glide panel that allows you to cross the cavern easily, but you must travel through thick mud that slows you down.

If you continue straight, you have a chance to collect an item box and gain Mini-Turbo boosts by hopping over the bumps in the road. Just be careful to avoid the geysers!

Dropping a Banana just after the geysers before the finish line is a great tactic for throwing off your opponents. They may not see the Banana as the geyser goes down until it's too late!

Mirror Mode

Take each turn in the opposite direction when you race along this flipped track!

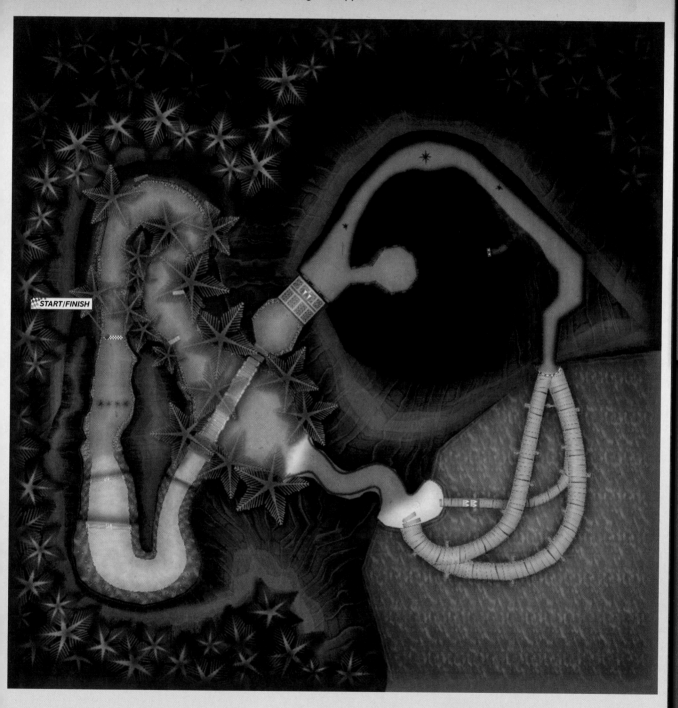

START/FINISH

DS Airship Fortress

Lightning Cup

There are a few dash panels along the track, but your drifting ability will determine your success. Dodge enemies, avoid collisions, and charge as many Mini-Turbos as possible. You won't find many shortcuts here, so keep your speed up!

ROAD HAZARDS

STEEP DROPS: Most of the track is surrounded by walls and fences, but steer clear of any damaged areas.

BANZAI BILLS: Watch out for incoming Banzai Bills; these oversized enemies pack a punch.

ROCKY WRENCHES: These troublemakers pop out when you least expect it. If you spot one of their hiding places, try to avoid it.

CRATES: You can smash through a crate, but it isn't recommended. Steer around them to maintain your speed.

CUTTING TORCHES: Avoid these intense flames at all costs—the heat is too much for your kart to handle.

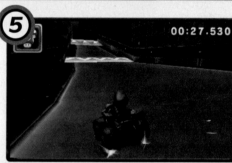

5   00:27.530

As soon as you pass by the cutting torches, begin a drift to the left. You should have enough time to get a Mini-Turbo boost before reaching the dash panels ahead of you.

6   00:34.891

Immediately after landing from your glide to the tower, start a drift to the left. Hold this drift until you reach the bottom of the tower. When you see the red-and-white arrows on the wall ahead of you, release the drift and begin a new drift to the right.

7   00:42.662

If done properly, you can get a Mini-Turbo boost from your last drift. As soon as you do, start a drift to the left and slide toward the wall away from the pit to the left. Use the coins to guide you in the direction in which to drift. Collect the two coins as you round the last corner before the finish line.

Time Trial

THE KART OF CHAMPIONS

 Character: Metal Mario

 Kart: Standard

Tires: Monster

Glider: Super Glider

2 00:12.330

Once you gain the boost from the dash panel, start drifting to the right. As you go around the corner, be careful to avoid the Rocky Wrenches that are all over the track. Release your boost where the track starts turning left.

3 00:14.957

Begin drifting to the left as you pass through the large doors. Continue holding the drift and collect any coins that cross your path. Release the drift for a Mini-Turbo boost as the course straightens out.

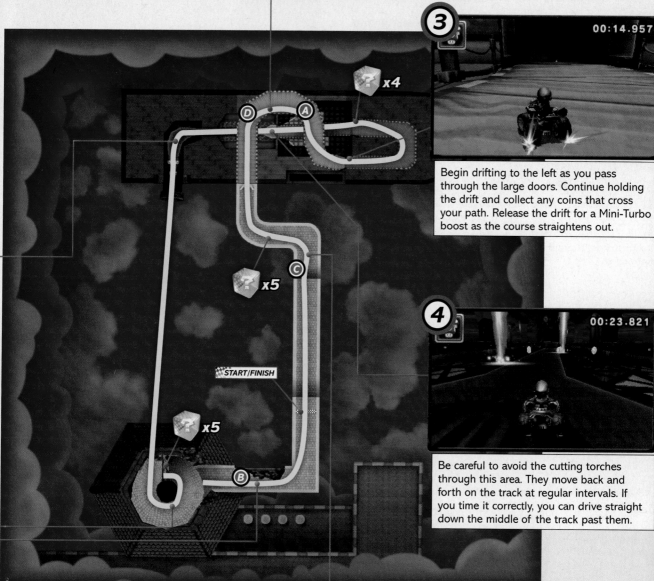

x4

x5

x5

START/FINISH

4 00:23.821

Be careful to avoid the cutting torches through this area. They move back and forth on the track at regular intervals. If you time it correctly, you can drive straight down the middle of the track past them.

1 00:05.561

From the starting line, continue straight down the track, avoiding any Banzai Bills that are heading toward you. At the first turn, drift left and release it just as you go around the corner. Immediately following the Mini-Turbo boost, begin drifting to the right. Release the drift when you are lined up with the dash panel ahead.

INTRODUCTION / NEW CUPS / CLASSIC CUPS / BATTLE MAPS

Tactics for Laps 2 and 3

Use the same basic tactics to complete the remaining laps. The Banzai Bills and Rocky Wrenches will keep you on your toes, but you shouldn't have any trouble dodging them.

Grand Prix

The section of track with all the Rocky Wrenches is a great place to drop a Banana. Adding an obstacle to an area that is already full of things to avoid is a great tactic to use against your opponents.

Dropping a Banana along the narrow section of track just before the finish line can make it very difficult for your opponents, especially if they are trying to drift through that area!

Take extra care when navigating the section with the Banzai Bills, especially with other racers around. You could find yourself being pushed right into one by an opponent!

If you have a Red Shell when you pass through the area with the Rocky Wrenches, save it! Don't use it in that area; it could accidently hit a Rocky Wrench instead of one of your opponents.

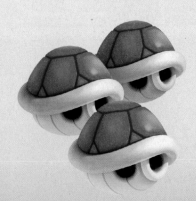

Mirror Mode

Once you've mastered the original course, apply what you've learned on this flipped track!

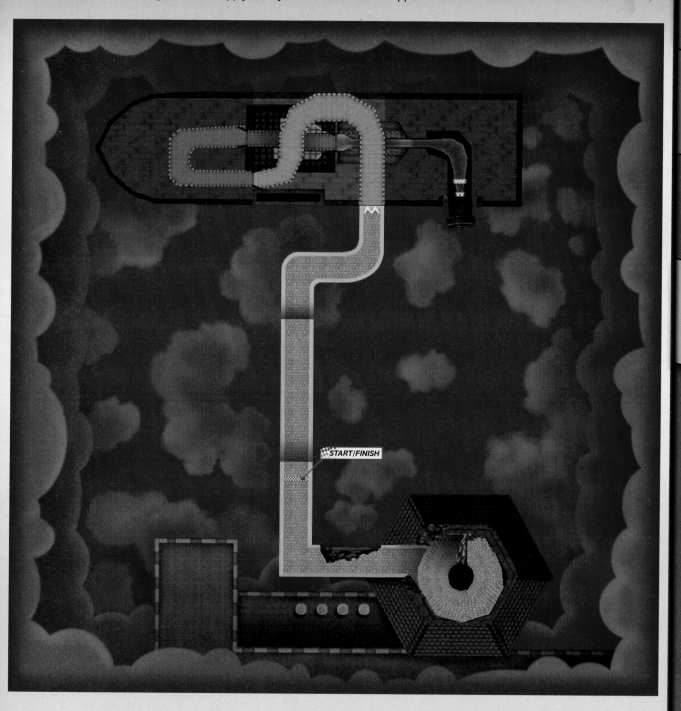

START/FINISH

SNES Rainbow Road

Lightning Cup

This course may look simple, but you're in constant danger of falling off the track. Drift through each turn, but make sure you stay in control of your kart. The Super Thwomps don't leave you much room to get around them, so you'll have to slip through some pretty tight gaps. Try to jump boost off the available ramps—just make sure you have a safe place to land!

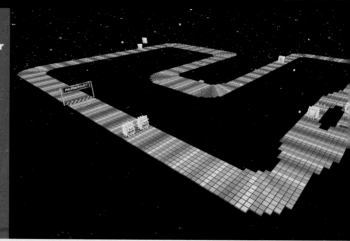

ROAD HAZARDS

 STEEP DROPS: Don't slip off this narrow track! Each fall will cost you precious time.

 SUPER THWOMPS: You don't want to get caught beneath a Super Thwomp when it comes crashing down. Plan your approach early to avoid swerving.

① 00:02.840

At the first turn following the starting line, drift to the right, making sure you stay as close to the edge as possible. Once you reach the straightaway, release your Mini-Turbo boost for a quick burst of speed toward the two Super Thwomps.

TIP

After a Super Thwomp hits the ground waves will appear on the track. Try to hop over them for a speed boost!

 **⑥ 00:13.102**

At the next turn, drift to the left and hold it until you see the long straightaway with a Super Thwomp at the end of it. As the Super Thwomp slams down on the track, it sends out ripples toward you. If you time it correctly, you can hop over each wave for a Mini-Turbo boost.

 **⑨ 00:27.434**

After landing from the jump, begin a drift to the right. As you round the corner, you will see another two Super Thwomps ahead of you. As you race for the finish line, keep your course to go directly in between each of the Super Thwomps. When you pass under them, you should see two shadows; as long as you stay out of those shadows, you will be safe.

 **⑧ 00:23.376**

Use a Mushroom as you approach the ramp that is between each of the Super Thwomps. Hop as you go over the green arrows on the ramp for an extra boost; this will help you reach the track on the other side.

Time Trial

THE KART OF CHAMPIONS

 Character: Lakitu

 Kart: Cloud 9

Tires: Roller

Glider: Paraglider

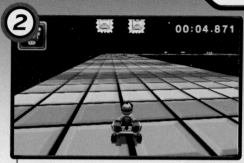

Drive directly between the two Super Thwomps as you go down the track. Make sure you have a shadow on either side of you as you go under them to avoid getting crushed!

After passing under the Super Thwomps, start a drift to the right and stay as close as you can to the edge without falling off. Hold this drift around the corner and try to collect as many coins as you can along the straightaway.

As you round the next corner, release your drift for a Mini-Turbo boost over the ramp ahead of you. Hop as you go over the ramp for another boost.

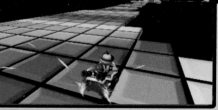

Drift around the next turn, staying close to the edge. Hold this drift until you are on a straightaway where you can see two Super Thwomps ahead of you. Keep driving forward where it looks like you are going to drop off the track.

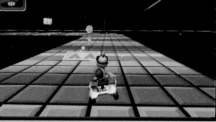

After jumping off the previous ramp, veer slightly to the left and jump over the next ramp. Again, hop as you go over the ramp for a speed boost.

INTRODUCTION

NEW CUPS

CLASSIC CUPS

BATTLE MAPS

Tactics for Laps 2 and 3

Use the same tactics to complete the remaining laps. Keep your turns smooth and your jumps true!

If you are passing an opponent who is near the track's edge, go ahead and bump them off!

Grand Prix

Dropping a Banana right in between Super Thwomps on this straightaway is a great strategy for throwing your opponents off, especially if it's the first lap!

Take extra caution if you have a Blooper used on you. On this track, it can be devastating to not be able to see your surroundings! Take your time and slow down just a bit; it's certainly better than falling off the track!

Be very careful when driving close to the track's edge! There are no guardrails on SNES Rainbow Road; all it takes is one mistake to fall off.

Mirror Mode

This mirrored track has all of the hazardous turns of the original course, but each of them is flipped!

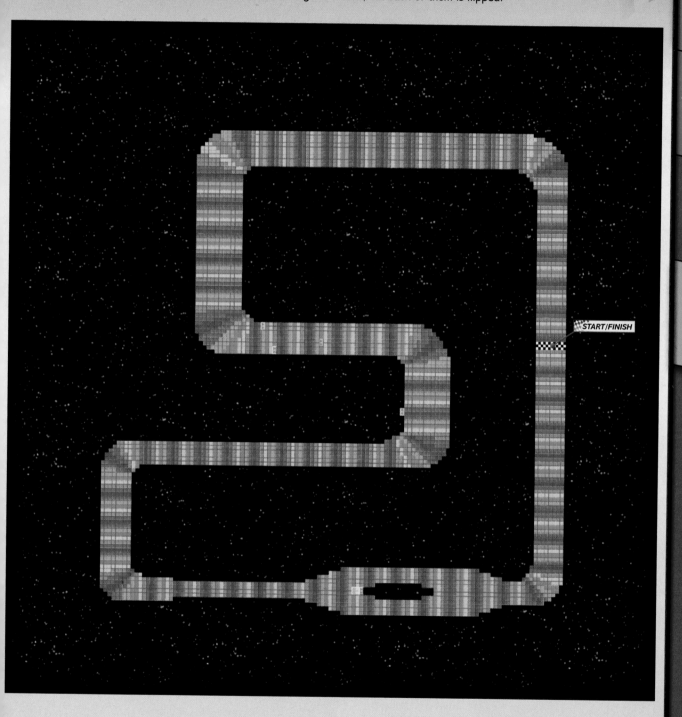

START/FINISH

Battle Maps

GBA Battle Course 1

Balloon Battle Tips

Watch out for the Rocky Wrenches around the course; if you run into one, you'll lose one of your balloons! Try to stay clear of them if you can. They are located between each of the colored areas.

Driving in the middle of the course can be very dangerous! You leave yourself wide open with no cover. Don't venture here unless you are feeling very brave or if you have a Star!

Coin Runner Tips

Perform a rocket start as the match begins. This will allow you to go straight for the single coin in the middle of the course. There is no risk involved since nobody will have an item yet. The only thing you have to worry about is a heavier character pushing you out of the way.

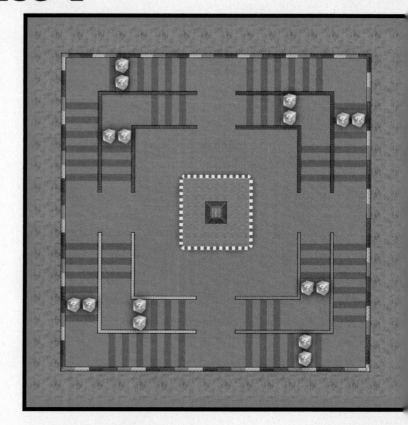

As you are grabbing coins, keep alternating between the outermost section of the course and the middle. Try not to stop! You'll be an easy target if you do, allowing your opponents to hit you with a Shell and take your coins.

DS Palm Shore

Balloon Battle Tips

As soon as the match begins, drive as fast as you can toward the middle island. This is the only place that you can find item boxes, and it is also the most dangerous spot to be! A good tactic is to get an item box and drive away quickly.

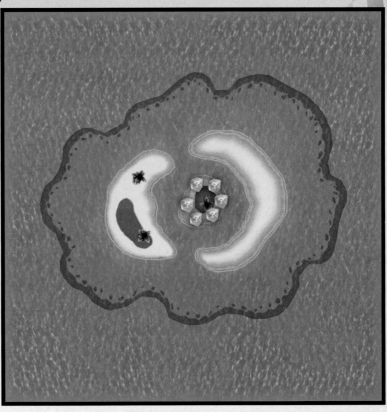

Watch out for the Sidesteppers all over the course! They wander and don't stay in the same location for long. If you run into one, you'll lose one of your balloons. They can be used defensively, though. If you see an opponent driving toward you with a Shell, hide behind a Sidestepper; it will take the hit instead of you!

Coin Runner Tips

While the track's outer portion is the safer area, you'll need to go back to the middle for more coins and items. As you pass through, be sure to find and throw a Shell at whoever has the highest amount of coins.

The trick in Coin Runners on this map is to get in and grab as many coins as you can, then drive toward the course's outer rim. The center island tends to get crazy with all the drivers constantly picking up items and just trading coins as they exchange hits.

N64 Big Donut

Balloon Battle Tips

During the match, glide panels appear occasionally around the middle ring. This can be a great escape from another player chasing you, and you have the added benefit of collecting an item box from the center of the course. Just be sure to pass over the air vent in the middle to make it to the other side!

If you ever find yourself being followed, pull a U-turn! There is plenty of room on this course to turn completely around and gain a mini boost from drifting. You can also use this tactic if an opponent passes you and you wish to turn around and chase them.

Coin Runner Tips

Keep an eye on the timer! If you have only a short amount of time to spare, choose coins over item boxes. Earlier in the match it is important to protect yourself, so try to balance collecting coins and getting items.

Keep moving on this course at all times. Don't stop for anything! Drift as you navigate the course to gain mini boosts.

Honeybee Hive
Balloon Battle Tips

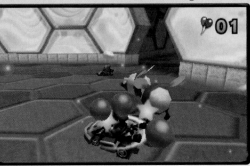

Watch out for the Stingbies on this course! They travel in a line of four and will pop one of your balloons if you run into them. They do move fairly slow, though, and can be used as cover from other drivers.

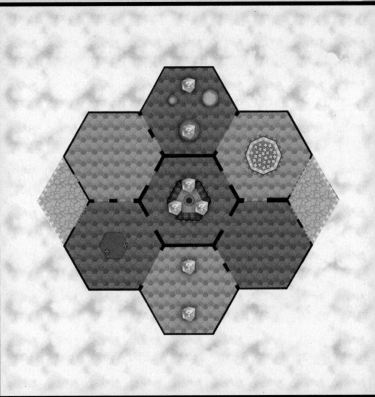

This course has a great getaway spot! If you ramp into the air vent in the very center of the course, it will launch you into the air and into one of the other rooms! This is a great way to escape your opponents.

Coin Runner Tips

While it may be very tempting to grab the item box, be aware that driving into the honey puddle will slow you down. This makes you an easy target for your opponents!

Staying out on the edges of the course can have benefits. Opponents chance falling off the edge if they try to ram you. You also have a good view of other drivers that head your way, giving you time to defend yourself with a Shell.

INTRODUCTION
NEW CUPS
CLASSIC CUPS
BATTLE MAPS

Sherbet Rink

Balloon Battle Tips

Stay out of the snow on this course; it will slow you down, making you an easy target! Stay more toward the outside of the course, though; going toward the middle allows your opponents to come at you from all angles!

Watch out for the penguins on the ice! They may look happy and friendly, but running into them will cost you a balloon. As with obstacles on the other courses, you can hide behind them for cover from your opponents.

Coin Runner Tips

The pink hearts and blue stars on the course won't stop you completely if you run into them; instead you will bounce off of them! While this isn't as bad as being stopped completely or spinning out, it will slow you down.

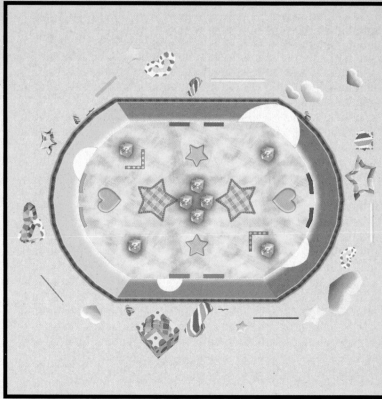

If you have the maximum ten coins and the time is almost out for the match, drive around the outside edge to stay away from everyone else! Try to keep a Shell or Banana on you for protection from the other drivers.

Wuhu Town

Balloon Battle Tips

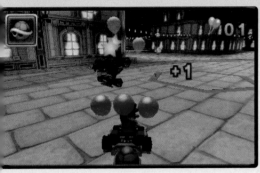

This course has quite a few different areas to navigate. A good tactic is to keep driving in and out of different streets through the town, picking up item boxes along the way. As you drive from one street to another, keep an eye out for other drivers who cross your path, and hit them with a Shell if they do!

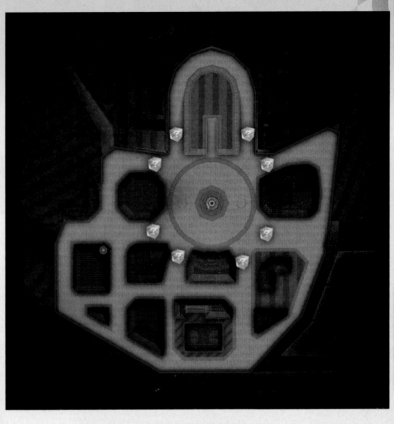

While hiding in the fountain may seem like a good idea, it isn't. Shells can still reach you here. No spot is completely safe from being hit, so always keep moving and watch the Touch Screen to know where your opponents are!

Coin Runner Tips

If you see several drivers battling around the fountain, drive by them quickly and scoop up all the coins that they are losing and escape! Just be ready, because the other racers may chase you down since you just took their coins!

When the clock is winding down to its final seconds, stay toward the outside of the course if you have a good number of coins. You may even come across a few more to get you to the maximum of ten.

Secret Checklists

Each time you unlock a secret, check it off of these lists. When you've checked off every item, you'll have uncovered all of the game's secrets!

GRAND PRIX CUPS

ICON	CUP	HOW TO UNLOCK
✓	Mushroom Cup	Unlocked by default
✓	Flower Cup	Place third or higher in the Mushroom Cup
✓	Star Cup	Place third or higher in the Flower Cup
✓	Special Cup	Place third or higher in the Star Cup
✓	Shell Cup	Unlocked by default
✓	Banana Cup	Place third or higher in the Shell Cup
✓	Leaf Cup	Place third or higher in the Banana Cup
✓	Lightning Cup	Place third or higher in the Leaf Cup
✓	Mirror	Place first in all cups in 150 cc

CHARACTERS

ICON		NAME	HOW TO UNLOCK
✓	M	Mario	Unlocked by default
✓	L	Luigi	Unlocked by default
✓	👑	Peach	Unlocked by default
✓	Yoshi	Yoshi	Unlocked by default
✓	Bowser	Bowser	Unlocked by default
✓	DK	Donkey Kong	Unlocked by default
✓	🍄	Toad	Unlocked by default
✓	🐢	Koopa Troopa	Unlocked by default
✓	🌼	Daisy	Place first in the Mushroom Cup in 150 cc
✓	W	Wario	Place first in the Flower Cup in 150 cc
✓	⭐	Rosalina	Place first in the Star Cup in 150 cc
✓	M	Metal Mario	Place first in the Special Cup in 150 cc
✓	😶	Shy Guy	Place first in the Shell Cup in 150 cc
✓	🐝	Honey Queen	Place first in the Banana Cup in 150 cc
✓	Wiggler	Wiggler	Place first in the Leaf Cup in 150 cc
✓	Lakitu	Lakitu	Place first in the Lightning Cup in 150 cc
✓	Mii	Mii	Place third or higher in the Special Cup and Lightning Cup in the same class

COIN COUNT

COINS	REWARD
☐ 50	Random part 1
☐ 100	Random part 2
☐ 150	Random part 3
☐ 200	Random part 4
☐ 250	Random part 5
☐ 300	Random part 6
☐ 400	Random part 7
☐ 500	Random part 8
☐ 600	Random part 9
☐ 700	Random part 10
☐ 800	Random part 11
☐ 900	Random part 12

COINS	REWARD
☐ 1,000	Random part 13
☐ 1,200	Random part 14
☐ 1,400	Random part 15
☐ 1,600	Random part 16
☐ 1,800	Random part 17
☐ 2,000	Random part 18
☐ 2,500	Random part 19
☐ 3,000	Random part 20
☐ 3,500	Random part 21
☐ 4,000	Random part 22
☐ 4,500	Random part 23
☐ 5,000	Random part 24

KARTS

ICON		NAME	HOW TO UNLOCK
✓		Standard	Unlocked by default
✓		Bolt Buggy	Unlocked by default
✓		Birthday Girl	Unlocked by default
✓		Egg 1	Collect coins from Grand Prix cups
✓		Tiny Tug	Collect coins from Grand Prix cups
✓		Cloud 9	Collect coins from Grand Prix cups
✓		Zucchini	Collect coins from Grand Prix cups
✓		B Dasher	Collect coins from Grand Prix cups

ICON		NAME	HOW TO UNLOCK
✓		Bruiser	Collect coins from Grand Prix cups
✓		Bumble V	Collect coins from Grand Prix cups
✓		Koopa Clown	Collect coins from Grand Prix cups
✓		Pipe Frame	Collect coins from Grand Prix cups
✓		Blue Seven	Collect coins from Grand Prix cups
✓		Cact-X	Collect coins from Grand Prix cups
✓		Barrel Train	Collect coins from Grand Prix cups
✓		Soda Jet	Collect coins from Grand Prix cups

TIRES

ICON		NAME	HOW TO UNLOCK
✓		Standard	Unlocked by default
✓		Monster	Unlocked by default
✓		Roller	Unlocked by default
✓		Slick	Collect coins from Grand Prix cups
✓		Slim	Collect coins from Grand Prix cups
✓		Sponge	Collect coins from Grand Prix cups
✓		Red Monster	Collect coins from Grand Prix cups
✓		Mushroom	Collect coins from Grand Prix cups
✓		Wood	Collect coins from Grand Prix cups

GLIDERS

ICON		NAME	HOW TO UNLOCK
✓		Super Glider	Unlocked by default
✓		Paraglider	Collect coins from Grand Prix cups
✓		Peach Parasol	Collect coins from Grand Prix cups
✓		Flower Glider	Collect coins from Grand Prix cups
✓		Swooper	Collect coins from Grand Prix cups
✓		Beast Glider	Collect coins from Grand Prix cups

GOLD PARTS

ICON		GOLD PART	HOW TO UNLOCK
✓		Gold Standard	Obtain a VR higher than 10,000 points or collect 20,000 coins
		Gold Tires	Earn a minimum one-star rating in every cup of each class or collect 15,000 coins
		Gold Glider	Connect with 100 people via StreetPass or collect 10,000 coins

ADDITIONAL SECRETS

SECRET	HOW TO UNLOCK
✓ Staff Ghost 1	Unlocked by default
Staff Ghost 2	Defeat Staff Ghost 1
✓ Creating Community	Play a Wi-Fi match
✓ Ending	Place third or higher in the Special Cup and Lightning Cup in the same class
True Ending	Place first in all cups in all classes
New title screen	Watch the True Ending
✓ One star near name	Obtain a one-star rating in all cups in all classes
Two stars near name	Obtain a two-star rating in all cups in all classes
Three stars near name	Obtain a three-star rating in all cups in all classes
Golden Steering Wheel	Play 100 recent matches and reach an 80 percent gyro usage rate (first-person camera)

PRIMA Official Game Guide
Written by Nick von Esmarch

Prima Games
An Imprint of Random House, Inc.

3000 Lava Ridge Court, Suite 100
Roseville, CA 95661
www.primagames.com

The Prima Games logo is a registered trademark of Random House, Inc., registered in the United States and other countries. Primagames.com is a registered trademark of Random House, Inc., registered in the United States. Prima Games is an imprint of Random House, Inc.

TM & © 2011 Nintendo. Nintendo properties are trademarks of Nintendo. © 2011 Nintendo. All Rights Reserved.

Product Manager & Co-Author: Jesse Anderson

Copyeditor: Carrie Andrews

Design & Layout: Elise Winter

Manufacturing: Stephanie Sanchez

Prima Games would like to thank: Emiko Ohmori, Yugo Sato, Kaori Yagi, Amanda Barrera, Andrew Best, Gordon Brown, Kriangkrai Buapetch, Christopher Hicks, Chris Huckins, Michael Sahlin, Michael Keough, and Noriyoshi Iwata.

All products and characters mentioned in this book are trademarks of their respective companies.

Important:
Prima Games has made every effort to determine that the information contained in this book is accurate. However, the publisher makes no warranty, either expressed or implied, as to the accuracy, effectiveness, or completeness of the material in this book; nor does the publisher assume liability for damages, either incidental or consequential, that may result from using the information in this book. The publisher cannot provide any additional information or support regarding gameplay, hints and strategies, or problems with hardware or software. Such questions should be directed to the support numbers provided by the game and/or device manufacturers as set forth in their documentation. Some game tricks require precise timing and may require repeated attempts before the desired result is achieved.

About the Author- Nick von Esmarch

Nick's obsession with gaming began in the days of 8-bit consoles and 1-button controllers. Born and raised in sunny California, Nick spent most of his childhood indoors, careful to avoid nearly all forms of social interaction. At the age of 22, he moved to Los Angeles to pursue opportunities in video game retail, eventually settling into a mildly successful acting career. Nick now spends all of his energy balancing acting and writing opportunities to support his fiercely defended gaming addiction.

ISBN 978-0-307-89384-0
Printed in the United States of America
11 12 13 14 LL 10 9 8 7 6 5 4 3 2 1